MW01046779

OUT OF THE SHADOWS

The Life of a CSE Canadian Intelligence Officer

BY RON LAWRUK

 **FriesenPress**

Suite 300 - 990 Fort St
Victoria, BC, Canada, V8V 3K2
www.friesenpress.com

Copyright © 2015 by Ron Lawruk
First Edition — 2015

All rights reserved.

No part of this publication may be reproduced in any form, or by
any means, electronic or mechanical, including photocopying,
recording, or any information browsing, storage, or retrieval
system, without permission in writing from the publisher.

Photo Credits:
Canadian and U.S. Vessels Participating in NATO Exercise
TEAMWORK 1980, Courtesy of RCN Forces;
TW-80 Team Photo, Author;
Author and Barbara Blaney Photos, Merla Lawruk
Images in the book will be shown at the end of each Chapter

ISBN
978-1-4602-6246-7 (Hardcover)
978-1-4602-6247-4 (Paperback)
978-1-4602-6248-1 (eBook)

1. Biography & Autobiography

Distributed to the trade by The Ingram Book Company

TABLE OF CONTENTS

*Resuming My Duties at CSE; CANUKUS Maritime
Intelligence Conference in Ottawa in1981 and
cancellation of 1982 Conference; Visit to GCHQ in
Cheltenham and British SIGINT Site at Scarborough
in 1982; Soviet SIGINT Reconnaissance/Spy vessels;
The World of Computers; CANUKUS Maritime
Intelligence Conference, London, England 1983; the
Dangers of Socializing; Golfing at Manderley Golf
Club; Muscular Dystrophy Charity Golf Tournament*

An Autobiography by Ronald N. Lawruk, former Intelligence Officer, who spent thirty-two years with the Communications Security Establishment (CSE), Canada, including 3 years at the U.S. National Security Agency (NSA) in Maryland, U.S.A

Portions of this manuscript have been submitted to the CSE and its counterpart organization at the U.S. National Security Agency (NSA). The information herein does not necessarily represent their agreement with the content, interpretation or veracity of the information. Names of CSE personnel were not used in. this book.

For my fellow CSE employees and their families, and to my family and close friends who trusted me, respected my rights and never asked any embarrassing questions.

Special thanks to my wife Merla, my first stage editor, for her valuable input, processing of photographs and slides, and especially her invaluable computer skills.

INTRODUCTION

For a good part of my working life I was employed as an Intelligence Officer at the Communications Security Establishment Canada (CSE), formerly the Communications Branch, National Research Council (CBNRC) between1958 and 1990.

You had to live during the time when Communism was escalating and becoming a major threat to Western countries to understand how the world was evolving. In the 1950s, Soviet spies were very active around the world and in Canada. The Communist expansion in Vietnam was threatening to spread to other Far East countries. The United States was sending an ever-increasing number of combat soldiers to the area.

Soviet Premier Nikita Krushchev pledged support for 'wars of national liberation'. Yet, opposition to Soviet rule by European countries like Romania, Hungary and Czechoslovakia was crushed with an iron fist.

In the late 1950s, Soviet bomber aircraft were conducting flights over the Arctic Ocean presumably to test the U.S./Canadian Distant Early Warning systems.

In 1960, U2 Pilot Gary Powers was shot down over the Soviet Union and the Cuban Missile Crisis brought the spectre of war to the North American continent. The Cold War was well underway.

In the late 1970s, the Soviets developed and expanded their Icebreaker Fleet, especially nuclear-powered icebreakers. The Fleet, which had one nuclear icebreaker in the 1960s, has grown into the largest icebreaking Fleet in the world. Many unclassified articles pertaining to these icebreakers and their capabilities and successes in the Arctic have been reported on the internet.

In the past few decades, the receding ice edge in the Arctic has made it easier for the Russians to operate, even conduct tourist trips to the North Pole. The Northern Sea Route, in the past restricted by perilous

Arctic ice conditions, could eventually be shifted north to the open ice areas. Trans-Arctic crossing times by Merchant convoys and inter –Fleet transfers of submarines and surface combat vessels, etc could be substantially shortened.

Icebreakers could also be used in support of Russian expansion of petroleum exploration in the high Arctic, Scientific Research expeditions, development of Russian communities and patrolling the Soviet portion of the Arctic soon to be defined by the International Law of the Sea Treaty.

It has become blatantly clear to me that once the boundaries of the Arctic are approved, the Soviets will be able to patrol and enforce their international boundaries and to escort and support Soviet surface and sub-surface Naval Forces operating anywhere in the Arctic Ocean.

In the past twenty-five years the Russians have released much information about their activities in the Arctic. This includes technological achievements in mapping the Arctic Ocean floor and the Hydrological, Meteorological and ice conditions. 'Open source' unclassified information released by Soviet scientists conducting research in the Arctic also had military and economic significance.

By way of comparison, Canada showed interest in the Soviet nuclear icebreakers in 1976, and as of 2014, has not replaced the ageing forty-five year old diesel-powered Louis St Laurent.

CSE was first established as the Canadian Government's National Cryptology Centre in 1946 as the Communications Branch under the umbrella of the National Research Council (CBNRC). Its role was to monitor foreign signals intelligence (SIGINT) and to protect Canada's Communications and Electronic data.

The unclassified Information Kit released by CSE[1] and updated in 2013 contained a section on SIGINT stating: "During the Cold War, the Establishment's primary client for SIGINT was the Canadian Department of National Defence and its focus was on the military operations of the then-Soviet Union.[2] Since the end of the Cold War, Government of Canada requirements have evolved to include a wide variety of

---

1   Internet; Communications Security Establishment Canada (CSE) Information Kit, modified 2013-06-27,

2   Jeffrey T Richelson and Desmond Ball. 'The Ties That Bind', Harper Collins 1986

political, defence and security issues of interest to a much broader range of client departments."

Working at CSE from the late 1950s to the 1990s was affected not only by the Cold War but also the shifting intelligence targets, the advances in military firepower, and the changes in technology, especially in the computer world.

The Cold War meant stringent controls over our private lives when it came to talking about our work. Nothing could be said. No one could be told – period!

To come home from work every day and not speak about where you worked or what you did was frustrating. When entertaining my neighbours, they must have thought I was a boor never to discuss anything remotely associated with my job.

That changed in 1974 when CSE was exposed and tagged as a "Canadian Spy Agency". From that point on, in the eyes of our families and friends, we were, unjustifiably, elevated to a "James Bond" level.

We still didn't discuss our work; it wasn't necessary. Everyone 'knew who we were and imagined what we did'. It took some of the pressure off, but we still had to keep our thoughts and opinions to ourselves when it related to anything involving CSE.

Until 1989, when the Berlin Wall came down and the Warsaw Pact began to dissolve, the most significant targets of the Democratic nations in the world were the Soviet Union and its Warsaw Pact partners (Bulgaria, Czechoslovakia, East Germany, Hungary, Poland and Romania); China and North Korea.

The main goal of intelligence agencies in the west, headed by the United States with partners in Australia, Canada, the United Kingdom, and New Zealand was to establish a unified method of collecting and exchanging SIGINT information on subjects and targets of mutual interest.

Canada was responsible for reporting on foreign operations along its coastline and territorial waters, and because of its proximity to Russia, all Soviet activities in the Arctic. This also included threats by international terrorists, drug runners, illegal aliens, etc. Real-time reporting was vital to provide our partners and our customers with current information on military, economic, scientific and diplomatic activities.

Being employed in the Western intelligence community, I quickly understood that it was important to identify your enemies and to know the location and capabilities of their troops and their weapons. That information, and the fact that they were aware that they faced immediate counter-attacks and potential nuclear annihilation, would go a long way towards keeping Democratic countries reasonably safe.

Of course, it was well known that these same target countries also had their own agendas and used their embassies abroad to collect intelligence on us.

Having witnessed the infiltration and successful penetration of Soviet spies into the Manhattan Project nuclear program and the Cambridge Spy Ring into the British intelligence organizations in the 1950s, we had to believe that there was a potential spy around every corner and possibly within CSE itself.

'Classified' and 'Need-to-know', two popular phrases, required the classification of different levels of information into Secret, Top Secret and Top Secret Codeword designators. These limited access restrictions were not appreciated by those who were unaware of the consequences when classified information and/or sources were revealed:

– the risk of damage to ongoing intelligence operations and the safety of the soldiers/civilians involved, and

– the loss of valuable and irreplaceable contacts/sources or a vital communications target

Things began to change in the 1990s with the collapse of the Warsaw Pact and the introduction of the Access to Information Act.

Technology developments, from the written hand-processed records to punch cards, readers and printouts in the 1950s, gave way to storage on large discs, magnetic tapes and automated systems. Today's CRAY super computers and sophisticated methods of handling, transmitting and storing information are a far cry from the day I joined the organization.

In the fifty-six years since I began working at CSE (including the twenty-four years since my retirement), the world of intelligence has changed. Russia is still a formidable adversary and other Communist countries like China and North Korea have become major threats to the world's stability both economically and militarily.

Terrorists have expanded their areas of influence to the Middle East, Asia and Africa and successfully targeted the U.S., the U.K. Canada and other countries in the world.

My wife Merla and I visited CSE in 2011 at an Open House for former employees and their families. The Sir Leonard Tilley building, where I worked for most of my career, had changed and was augmented by a new structure, the Edward Drake Building (Ed Drake was the Chief of CBNRC when I first joined the organization).

During our 2011 visit, we were briefed by young employees of CSE who described the present day role and activities (the sanitized version, I would assume) of the organization. They also showed us the design of the new CSE facility which would be built close to the CSIS (Canadian Security and Intelligence Services) in the east end of Ottawa.

During our tour of the CSE Watch Centre, we were also briefed on the methods used to monitor current developments and/or threats to Canada and its Allies. Having served some time as an Intelligence Briefer to the Chief of CSE and his Senior Staff in CSE's SIGINT Operations Centre in the late 1980s, I could see how the fusion of CSE and CSIS would improve the coverage of threats to our country and speed up the reaction time.

I was pleased to learn that we were supporting Canadian troops on peace-keeping missions. It was a natural transition to feed real-time and crucial intelligence to our service personnel in these areas. In the late 1980s, I had briefed various Canadian military staff at North American and European sites on this potential and essential service.

Our visit also confirmed my belief that the SIGINT world has changed. Technology and computerization have again evolved beyond the rudimentary methods we employed while I still worked in CBNRC/CSE.

Collection of intelligence information from Morse code and to some extent radio communications has, I assume, been replaced by more advanced technology. Staffing at our intercept sites has been reduced since the introduction of remoting methods.

Communications have become so sophisticated; it now only takes milliseconds, not days to exchange information with our partners, consumers and military forces.

We were warned to be careful and selective about 'Disinformation' which could lead us down the wrong path and distort our order-of-battle records.

Though spies and counter-spies had been detected in England and the U.S., during my years in the intelligence field, I was never aware of any spies being uncovered in CSE.

Recently, the worldwide internet has spawned a backlash by various media organizations and the public about the NSA defector Edward Snowden's revelations concerning Government agencies spying on innocent civilians. Articles referred to: 'Canada's Secret Metadata Surveillance

Activities'[3]; 'Who's Watching the Watchers?'[4] and 'Canada Has NSA Style Surveillance System'[5].

I would like to ask a question of those who accuse the intelligence community of invading their privacy: "What would you think if an experienced officer of a government agency had picked up a conversation between two people about bombing the Twin Towers in New York? If your children were visiting their father at one of the buildings and the officer found out in time to get them out, would you be so critical? Would you still feel that it was an invasion of your privacy or would you support and thank them for their efforts?"

As I began to write this book, I realized that I had to come to grips with the reality of my situation. CSE was not going to be pleased with the possibility that one of their former employees would be publishing a 'tell-all' autobiography - the first to do so. I assumed that they hoped that I would give up or just disappear.

When describing events or situations which they might consider too revealing, sensitive and embarassing to the organization and to my fellow employees, I knew that I would have to be careful. I was well aware that the types of situations that I considered to be funny or comical in the 1950s, and up to the 1980s, might not seem so amusing in the 21st Century.

Another factor came into play. In order to describe unusual or 'zany' situations, I would need the approval of former employees or their families. Since many were deceased, I decided not to include those anecdotes in my book.

I was also well aware of the fact that the current staff of CSE was under considerable duress because of the Edward Snowden 'revelations'. It was a difficult time to thrust this additional burden on CSE for reviewing my book. However, I had to consider my age (80) and the 24 years since my retirement. Also, considering the world situation in 2014 (the Soviet activity in the Ukraine and the ISIS threat in the Middle East), I had to face the fact that the release of my book was timely.

My research on the Internet bolstered my decision to go forward. To this end, I decided to use the plethora of unclassified reports from Russian

---

3   Globe and Mail, 1 May 2014

4   National Post, 10 Oct 2013

5   Huffington Post, 10 June 2013

and other open source reports available on the Internet since 1990. Many articles had also been released by the western Intelligence Agencies pertaining to their operations in the Arctic between the 1950s and the 1990s, and into the 21st Century.

The timing was right.

Screening and Approval by CANUKUS Agencies

The draft of this book was provided to CSE Staff who screened the contents on behalf of the U.S. National Security Agency (NSA) and the British Government Communications Headquarters GCHQ). I wanted to ensure that the information herein did not affect my responsibility to adhere to the Official Secrets Act which I had signed when I retired from the organization.

I provided CSE with a brief outline of my first manuscript in the summer of 2012.

On 26 October 2012, I received a copy of an unclassified letter from NSA stating that they had "no objection to the public release of this document as written. They also added that "nothing in this notice of approval should be construed to indicate that the information included in this manuscript is factually accurate".

Between October 2012 and June 2014, I had regular e-mail/telephone exchanges with, and personal visits to CSE pertaining to the contents of the book.

On 4 June 2014, I met with CSE staff and was presented with a revised copy of my manuscript containing their suggested changes to my latest draft. I was told that the copy was now considered "Unclassified". I was allowed to carry it out of the building and through the Guard house without an envelope.

I made all of the final changes as requested by CSE to the areas they had marked and forwarded them to CSE staff as an attachment to my 9 June e-mail.

On 27 June 2014, I received a letter from the Director General, Policy and Communications at CSE stating, " We have reviewed the latest version you provided, and we appreciate the changes you made to the book, and the care you took in making them. I would like to thank you for your patience, understanding and cooperation over the last several months and wish you good luck in publishing your book."

I am truly convinced that CSE must protect its sources and its methodology in order to identify and thwart those who would harm us. The safety of our troops, intelligence officers and embassy staffs abroad and the security of our citizens are paramount.

This is not meant to be an expose' of the CSE nor intended to reveal secrets which would undermine the valuable work being done by dedicated staff to protect the country we love so dearly.

Moreover, the information used in this manuscript is my interpretation of the facts as I saw them. In some cases I have attempted to determine the reasons for previously unexplained activities noted during my years of service with CSE. Though most of the information seems to fit the activity and time-frame, it doesn't necessarily provide the only answer.

It may appear to the reader that I have presented the Russians in a favorable light. That was certainly not my goal. Prior to 1990, I had little or no unclassified information available outside the Communications Intelligence community.

The Soviet aggression in the Ukraine in the spring of 2014 had a profound effect on me. 100 years ago, in 1914, my grandmother, carrying nothing but clothing, some bread and vegetables fled the oncoming Russian hordes She was accompanied by her mother-in-law, my father (two years old) and my uncle (four years old). She joined her husband who had gained employment at a lumber camp just outside of Ottawa, Canada. They never again saw their family or friends in the Ukraine.

While the aggression in the Ukraine was well advertised in 2014, Russian plans for the development and protection of their Arctic sector was gaining momentum. President Putin was preparing to defend the new territorial boundaries of the Arctic to be designated by the Law of the Sea Treaty. To this end, a new military base was established on an island north of the Russian mainland. A flotilla of the most powerful nuclear icebreakers in the world escorted Soviet naval vessels through the receding ice cover in an area in the high Arctic.

In my opinion, these events, coupled with the increasing development of the Soviet petroleum industry in the Arctic, indicates that Putin means business.

Due to the number of abbreviations and acronyms used, I have included a listing at the end of the book. For readers who are unfamiliar with the locations of cities and geographical sites in the Arctic, I would recommend the use of an Atlas.

ONE

1980, Atlantic Ocean - A strong wind blew across the Nova Scotia coastline as the storm headed out to sea. A flash of lightning illuminated the gray hull of the Canadian destroyer. The HMCS *Athabaskan*, lifted by the gigantic waves, rose eight metres then slid down the slope like a bobsled on an icy Olympic run.

On the Bridge, the Captain stared into the bleak darkness of the blustery cold September night and grimaced as conditions worsened. He was worried that the heavy weather and high seas would hinder the operation and affect the outcome.

The First Officer shouted out, "Maintain course, speed twenty knots."

The Captain scanned the information he had been given, "Target One, line bearing straight ahead, Target Two at line bearing thirty-five degrees to starboard."

He repeated the information to the navigator who steered the ship towards a position between the two readings. He realized that he had reluctantly placed his ship in the hands of the CSE Signals Intelligence (SIGINT) team two decks below.

The SIGINT team, which I headed, included members from the Canadian Forces Supplementary Radio System (CFSRS) from the Canadian Forces Station (CFS) at Leitrim, Ontario, Canada. The inclusion of our CSE/CFSRS team and Maritime Command Headquarters (MARCOMHQ) staff in an ongoing operation (see image 1) was the first example of a combined Canadian intelligence mission in support of a NATO Exercise, TEAMWORK-80 (see image 2).

The *Athabaskan*, a Helicopter –carrying Destroyer (DDH 282) was the command ship of the Canadian Fleet, the 'Orange Team' during the NATO Exercise. Its role was:

"To penetrate the protective shield of U.S. 'Blue Team' vessels escorting the Nuclear –Powered Aircraft Carrier (USSN) *Nimitz* undetected and come within firing distance of the nuclear-powered goliath."

Our suggestion that the Captain turn off all of the *Athabaskan's* radar and electronic equipment and operate in radio silence did not sit well with him at first. We convinced him that it was the only way he could successfully complete this part of the exercise task.

We were facing heavy seas and high winds while the storm raged above. As I sat beside the radio operator below deck and relayed information to the Captain, I had time to think about my luck at being involved in such an exciting occupation.

In March 1958, I answered an ad in The Ottawa Citizen for a clerical position at the National Research Council of Canada. The NRC had a reputation for being one of the top organizations with which to be employed in the Ottawa area. At that time, the most important advantage of working in the Canadian Government was job security. I sent in my letter including my CV, listing my employment history and was given an interview.

"I noticed in your application that your father is Ukrainian", said the woman interviewer. "Do you speak the language or any other language?"

"No, unfortunately for me, my father only spoke the language with his mother. My mother was French. She still speaks it, but my parents only spoke English with my two sisters and I."

"Would you be interested in learning to speak the language, if given the opportunity?"

"Sure. I would love to learn. Perhaps it would help me to speak with my Grandmother when she visits us."

"I noticed that you moved to Calgary last year and returned to Ottawa. It seemed kind of sudden. What was the reason?"

I had anticipated this question.

"I was an accountant/bookkeeper with Spartan Air Services in Ottawa since 1952. In 1957, after completing a competition for an Office Manager/Accountant position in one of their new branches in Kenya or Calgary, I was selected."

I had been following the news from Kenya where the tribal conflicts were becoming ever more violent. The Mau-Mau tribe was hacking white people to death. I quickly ruled out that venue and chose Calgary. I was also getting married in June of that year."

"My wife and I moved to Calgary in July 1957. She became pregnant and was not happy living so far away from her family. I enjoyed my job but knew that I would have to decide which was more important."

The interviewer smiled at me and said, "Well, Mr. Lawruk, I can't tell you any more at this time. The RCMP will be conducting a background search and will probably be interviewing your friends and neighbours. It could take two to three months. If you're successful, we would be willing to offer you an annual salary of $3200 a year."

I don't know where the courage came from. I knew that now I had a family to support and dared to overcome my shyness. I replied, "I was hoping to get $3500. That's what I was being paid by Spartan."

"I'll enter that on the interview form. Good luck."

As I drove home, I thought about the interview. Considering the emphasis on the unique language requirements, I had my doubts. I anguished at the foolishness of asking for more money. After all, I was only working part-time and when I was in high school, I dropped Latin from my curriculum!

In the spring of 1952, when I was only eighteen years old, I was attending St. Patrick's College in Ottawa, Ontario, Canada, finishing off my Junior Matriculation in Grade Twelve and taking a few classes in Grade Thirteen. As a starting 'forward' on the St. Pats Senior Basketball Team, I was hoping to get into a University where I could continue to play and get some type of degree.

My marks were not encouraging. When I dropped Latin, it ended my dream of being a lawyer, so I shifted my emphasis to become an Accountant. I wasn't expecting the event which would change my life forever.

A priest at St. Pats advised my parents that it would be better for me to look for a full time job that coming summer. The cost of University was well beyond their means and he could get me a well paying job.

The company, an aerial photography firm, Spartan Air Services, had tremendous potential. It was being run by young men, including fixed wing and helicopter pilots. One of the most famous was 'Weldy' Phipps, a renowned Canadian bush pilot.

Spartan was equipped with many war-surplus aircraft such as P38s, Mosquitos, Cansos, DC3s and Sea Hornets. The company performed high altitude photography and magnetometer surveys not only in Canada, but around the world. Mapping in Northern Canada was used to assist in the establishment of the Distant Early Warning System – the DEW line in Canada.

I began work at Spartan in June 1952. I was shy, introverted and 'wet behind the ears'. I worked my way up the ladder from a Junior Bookkeeper to an Assistant Accountant. Because I was responsible for making up the monthly payroll, I knew most of the Ottawa staff and made a lot of friends in the company. We had a profit sharing plan. Many employees with long service received hefty bonus cheques at Christmas time.

I was very upset when we lost two P-38s which crashed in the Ottawa Area in 1955. Around that time Spartan had about sixty aircraft, twenty-five Fixed Wing and thirty-five Helicopters.

My wife and I arrived in Calgary in July 1957 during the Calgary Stampede. I was greeted by the General Manager and the Head of the Photographic Unit and at the age of twenty-three, immediately assumed responsibility for the Accounting and Office functions.

We had regular working breakfasts every Monday morning. I also took inventory on aircraft parts, aerial photography equipment and general stock. The GM and I travelled to Edmonton on business and to check out our inventory there.

I loved the mountains, the scenery and the weather. My wife and I made trips to Banff, the Columbia Glacier and Lake Louise. What spectacular sights!

On one occasion, when we were involved in a topographic survey, a combined aerial and ground operation along the Banff railroad, I went along with the ground crew. One of the guys drove up to Banff in his MG convertible sports car.

After completing our survey chores one day, we decided to go for a drive through the mountains. When we turned onto a dirt road, there in front of us was an enormous moose. From my seat in the MG he looked twelve feet tall. He must have thought we were a couple of bugs. We 'high-tailed' it out of there in no time.

From the outset, my wife was not happy. We both wanted children and she had become pregnant. She had a bad fall while she was five months pregnant and that compounded the problem.

A couple of months later, things were also happening on the operational front. Spartan's fortunes were waning. They had lost a few aircraft and their shares dropped. With an unhappy pregnant wife and Spartan's bleak outlook, I decided to move back to Ottawa. It was a tough decision for me, but I felt it was the right one.

4

I soon secured a part time bookkeeping job with an associated firm, Canadian Aero Service, and spent three months there before the National Reseach Council interview.

Spartan eventually declared bankruptcy but maintained the helicopter operations in Calgary.

1. NATO Exercise TEAMWORK-80 SIGINT Team

2. Canadian/U.S.Convoy TW-80

TWO

Aboard the HMCS *Athabaskan* - As the Canadian vessels moved southeast into the Atlantic Ocean and closed on the shield of American vessels protecting the Aircraft Carrier *Nimitz*, I recalled the first time I heard about the NATO exercise Teamwork-80.

Teamwork-80 involved a number of Atlantic countries including the U.S., Canada, the U.K., the Netherlands and Norway to name a few. The operation would be carried out in the North Atlantic between the Azores and Norway.TW-80 was well advertised by the participating NATO countries. The Soviets were known to deploy a few naval combatant vessels to these exercise sites and sometimes interfered with the operations.

Participating Canadian vessels included the destroyer *HMCS Athabaskan* (DDH282), *HMCS Ottawa* (DDH229), *HMCS Assiniboine* (DDH234) and the Auxiliary Oil Replenishment ship *HMCS Protecteur* (AOR509). The U.S. Fleet Commander was on the U.S. nuclear aircraft carrier, the *USSN Nimitz* (CVN68).

In September 1980, I met the Canadian Forces Supplementary Radio System (CFSRS) team before we boarded the flight to Halifax. The senior member, a Sergeant, and I knew each other. In Halifax, I stayed in the Officer's Quarters; the radio operators from CFSRS were billeted at the base.

I got a lot of ribbing from the team about that. We loosened up at a local bar where I met each of the members of the team.

The next day I had scheduled a meeting with the appropriately-cleared Maritime Command (MARCOM) HQs staff in Halifax to discuss the upcoming mission and to brief them on my recent appointment in CSE.

I also met the two members of MARCOM staff, who would accompany us on the mission. I described CSE's role in support of their overall operations and outlined our mission during TEAMWORK-80. They briefed us on Canada's responsibilities and their role in relation to TW-80.

At the quay where all of the ships were moored, I was surprised when I first saw the HMCS Athabaskan, the Command Ship for the Canadian contingent during the exercise. To a landlubber, the sides of the Destroyer looked like cardboard pasted to the hull. I was going into the North Atlantic where the waves and swells measured twenty to thirty feet high!

We were escorted onto the ship and introduced to the Captain, the First Officer and the Supply Officer.

Arrangements had been made for me to stay in the Supply Officer's quarters which had two beds; the CFSRS team was billeted with the crew members.

While the ship prepared to leave port, the CFSRS Team Leader and I met with the other members of the team and discussed our role and duties in support of TW-80. We would work normal hours until we encountered Warsaw Pact vessels or aircraft or were required to support the Captain in any 'friendly' operation. We set up shifts to ensure twenty-four hours coverage of their communications.

We also advised the Captain and his staff that we would require an area to ensure security measures concerning our equipment and conversations.

The crew of the Athabaskan seemed puzzled by our presence. They had been informed that we would be performing special operations and couldn't discuss it with anyone. Our working area below deck was off limits to them and we could detect some negative reactions to our presence.

I was dressed in civilian clothes (with the checkered pants in the photo) and the ship's crew must have regarded me as an intruder at first. Some may have even thought that I was spying on them à la CIA! Since none of them had ever heard of CSE, that may have been the reason for their standoffish behavior. I couldn't blame them.

I could imagine how they felt when we put up sheets across our work area and totally hid the radio position.

We found our working space very small for a three shift/six-man-team, but they managed to give us as much room as they could spare. When I saw where the CFSRS team was quartered, I never complained about my situation. One of the guys had to sleep with his head a few inches below the pipes from the bulkhead.

I was concerned about getting seasick. The stench of oil permeated the air and mingled with the various smells of food from the galley.

However, one of the crew shared the secret to avoiding sea sickness: eat lots of soda crackers. Good advice. I never got sick.

I ate with the Officers. The food from the galley was quite good and I gather that the CFSRS team members were also satisfied with the variety and quality. I never heard any complaints. We were also advised to remove our rings while onboard the ship. As one stepped through the passages between decks, a ring could catch on the steel edges and possibly rip one's finger off.

We stood on the deck as the *Athabaskan* moved out of Halifax Harbour and passed the downtown development areas and the houses along the shore. People waved to us from both sides. The channel was calm, dark clouds were moving in and rain was forecast.

The CFSRS Team Leader and I met with the Commander, the Captain and the First Officer to get a briefing on TW-80 and determine what they needed from us during ongoing operations.

They explained the various phases of the NATO exercise, the areas of operations and their role in the upcoming NATO 'Friendly Orange/ Blue' exercise. The 'Blue' Forces led by the Nuclear Aircraft Carrier *USSN Nimitz* was leaving the U.S. Atlantic Fleet naval base at Norfolk, Virginia and heading northeast across the Atlantic towards the Azores.

The 'Orange' team headed by the *Athabaskan* would attempt to infiltrate the U.S. Fleet and get within 'deadly fire' range of the *Nimitz* which was being escorted by a large fleet of destroyers, frigates and supply ships.

The Canadian squadron would have to penetrate the shield around the *Nimitz* undetected. If detected, the Canadian Fleet Commander would be notified and the Canadian vessels would have been deemed destroyed. However, if any Canadian vessel got within firing range of the *Nimitz* undetected, it would be considered a victory for the 'Orange Team'.

Once the *Athabaskan* entered the Atlantic, we began our search for transmissions involving units of the U.S. vessels. Our radio operators said that the Americans were constantly chatting on circuits that we could easily monitor and were either complacent or unconcerned, or didn't consider the Canadian Fleet a serious threat.

The First Officer informed us that there was a storm in the area and operating in close proximity to the American vessels would be very risky without the use of our radar. We advised him that the teams on the American vessels could easily pinpoint our vessel and 'destroy' us before we got within range of the *Nimitz*.

We outlined what our team's capabilities and limitations were with respect to radio reception in the North Atlantic area of operations.

The biggest problem was that, in order for the Canadian vessels to get close to the U.S. Fleet, all electronics would have to be shut down. Our team discussed that problem and offered a solution. The ship would have to operate under visual conditions and depend solely on our 'line bearing' information. As long as the American operators continued to chat, we could provide the line bearings on each of the vessels.

The Commander appeared pleased and agreed with our plan. The electronics were shut down. Now here we were, approaching the first U.S. destroyers responsible for protecting arguably the world's most powerful and destructive vessel.

The storm grew worse. It was to our advantage that we could not be detected visually and we weren't communicating. That offered us some relief.

All of our efforts were placed in one basket: the efficiency of our operators. The other concern we had was the capability of the *Athabaskan's* crew to steer clear of the area around the destroyers protecting the *Nimitz* during the storm with limited visibility.

Working in shifts, the CFSRS leader and/or I sat beside the radio operator. The verbose U.S. radiomen continued to chat on the open circuits about their jobs, families, and the latest sports scores. In my opinion, they appeared to be oblivious to our presence, complacent about our capability to effectively penetrate their shield and, strange as it seemed, disinterested.

As we moved closer to the vessels protecting the *Nimitz*, everyone was on edge. The Captain had placed all of his trust, in the direction of the ship, to this unknown group, snidely referred to by some of the crew as 'Spooks'. These were tense moments as we closed in on the first two American vessels.

We felt that it had to work. We had no choice. In the back of my mind was the thought, "If we fail, would that be the end of joint ventures in support of a real live operation by the Canadian Navy?"

That question was quickly answered. We had successfully passed undetected between two widely-separated American convoy vessels. We were now inside the 'protective shield' around the *Nimitz* and had isolated the speaker on the aircraft carrier's radio.

Now, we had to move close enough to the *Nimitz* to switch on all of our radio and electronic equipment and reveal our location. You could see the relief on all of our faces and, from what we were later told, the grins on the officers on the bridge of the *Athabaskan*.

While still some distance away but within firing range of the U.S. aircraft carrier, the Captain gave the order, "Switch on all electronic equipment including radars and send a message to the *Nimitz*."

I had hoped it would have included the word - 'Gotcha'.

The Fleet Commander and Maritime Headquarters in Halifax were advised that our TW-80 exercise was successful; the Orange Forces had infiltrated the Blue Forces and were in range to attack the *Nimitz*.

The Canadian Commander, the Captain and First Officer were delighted with the result. Our level of credibility and respect was elevated with the crew of the *Athabaskan*.

From that time on, we were treated as teammates and became a 'Canadian Team'; the crew members were more cooperative and friendly for the remainder of our voyage. It made the rest of our mission in support of the convoy more satisfying.

I had time to reflect on how lucky I was to be involved in the operation and the day I became an Intelligence Officer.

THREE

On 27 April 1958, our first child was born at Montfort Hospital in Eastview (now Vanier). My wife Jacqueline and I were delighted. She was a healthy, beautiful girl that we named Debra Ann.

A month later, I received a letter on National Research Council letterhead stating that I had been accepted for a Research Clerk Two position with the Communications Branch of the National Research Council (CBNRC) at a salary of $3500.

I was ecstatic!

Little did I know about the world I was entering!

Following instructions in the letter, I drove to the CBNRC building on Alta Vista Drive in East Ottawa. It was an old stone building surrounded by a high chain-link fence located next to a small shopping centre. Originally a Grey Nuns Convent, it was also the site of the Rideau Military Hospital during World War Two.

I recognized the structure; my Dad had shown it to me a few years earlier. As a Sgt-Major in the Royal Canadian Army Medical Corps, he had been sent there to recuperate after one of his lungs was removed.

Security at CBNRC was very tight. I had to show my driver's licence and my letter from the Employment Officer. It turned out that she was the same person who interviewed me at the NRC.

After the usual discussion on administrative matters, she escorted me to the Security Office where I was given a short briefing by the Security Officer. He outlined the Official Secrets Act and witnessed my signature on the appropriate forms.

A short time later, he escorted me to the Training Officer. His job was to introduce me to the world of Intelligence. I entered a shadowy world about which few people even knew existed and a place in which even fewer would have access.

I was fascinated when he explained how the Canadian Intelligence organization was formed as an Examination Unit in June 1941 to intercept the communications of Germany and the Vichy in France. Subsequently, to hide its existence from Canada's enemies, it became a branch of NRC. In December 1945, the Examination Unit became the Communications Branch under the NRC umbrella, thus CBNRC.

The Training Officer emphasized that "we monitor the communications of countries which we consider enemies or a threat to Canada in order to protect our national security and to ensure that Government communications are secure".

He described the worldwide structure of the free world organizations known as AUSCANUKUSNZ. The countries of Australia, Canada, United Kingdom, United States and New Zealand had an agreement to share intelligence for the good of the Community. There was also an agreement that none of these countries would collect information on one another.

The U.S. organization was headed by the National Security Agency (NSA) and the British were represented by the Government Communications Headquarters (GCHQ), formerly Bletchley Park.

CBNRC provided specific Departments in the Canadian Government with Signals Intelligence (SIGINT) service gleaned from foreign countries considered to be targets by the AUS/CAN/UK/US/NZ community.

Canadian Department of National Defence requirements also included all foreign activities off the coast of Canada and in the Arctic. In the case of the Soviet Union that included any airborne activity in or near Canadian airspace.

He also outlined the unofficial but not the internationally-accepted boundaries in which each country claimed sovereignty over areas in the Arctic Ocean. Because of Canada's proximity to the northernmost hemisphere, "CBNRC is responsible for monitoring the activities of all foreign military organizations, the Navy, Army and Air Forces and their Air Defence systems, and any associated civil activity in support of their military."

He made particular mention of the Soviet capability to strike Canadian and northern U.S. cities over the North Pole using heavy bombers[6]. That thought certainly struck a nerve for me.

It took me some time to absorb everything he said. I was well aware of world events at that time. The Soviets were a major threat to the western world. It continued its iron-fist rule over countries it had assimilated during WWII, the occupation of East Germany, Hungary, Poland, Romania and Hungary.

Expansionism was rampant. The missile crisis in 1960 was just around the corner. The Soviets had planted numerous moles in British universities who would have a significant effect on the stability of the United Kingdom.

An NSA document released in November 2012 titled '60 Years of Defending Our Nation'[7] stated:

"During this time, the Soviet Union and its allies continued to be NSA's major concern. Cold War intelligence targets included Russian military forces, strategic rocket forces, air defense forces and airborne troops. In addition, commanders also sought intelligence on the other countries of the Warsaw Pact."

I soon learned why the CSE Employment Officer had asked me about my linguistic capabilities, and so much more.

"You will begin your training program by studying the geography of Russia, particularly the northern regions all the way to the North Pole. Familiarize yourself with the geographical features and locations of cities, towns and islands."

"You will also spend several hours a day learning the Russian language, the Cyrillic alphabet and Morse code. Later, you will learn how to break codes and transliterate messages."

He also emphasized the need for caution when interpreting the intelligence gleaned from Russian sources. The use of 'disinformation' was one of their tactics to thwart our intelligence on their locations and Order-of-Battle.

I listened with enthusiasm and wonderment. Until now, I had no idea about the world I was about to enter. I recognized the challenge it

---

6   **NORAD at 40, Historical Review: Soviet Long Range Aviation,Internet**

7   **NSA, 60 Years of Defending Our Nation, November 2012**

presented and had some doubts as to whether I could handle it. It was a new challenge but it sounded exciting.

"Remember, you are bound by the Official Secrets Act not to divulge anything about the organization, its activities and your work. You cannot tell your spouse, your family or friends. That will be one of your biggest challenges. If pressed, you can tell them that you are working in a classified area and can't discuss anything."

The drive home that first day was exhilarating but I also realized it could become very stressful. Everyone would want to know more about my new job and what I did.

It was very frustrating. Everyone would know that I was being evasive, secretive. I couldn't tell them a thing. Once I mentioned that the job was classified, I couldn't elaborate.

There was no one to talk to, except my co-workers. I would learn later that in some instances, because I was given access to 'special material', I could only converse with my co-workers if they too had the same clearances. My wife and my parents never pressed me about it. To their inquisitive friends they innocently said with a touch of sarcasm: "We don't know what Ron does - some secret hush-hush job at the Research Council. You know. All of those scientists at the NRC."

Two weeks later, I was assigned to my first job involving Foreign Air Operations in the Arctic. At first, all I did was sort stacks of 'intercepted messages' into chronological order for the Senior analysts.

Some of my fellow recruits initially had trouble accepting the task of reading messages involving foreign military personnel. I understood what could be interpreted from these exchanges and how it could aid our cause. Occasionally, a lonely soldier would inadvertently mention his location and/or his unit's movements to another base.

The information we gleaned would never be directly harmful to the Soviet people involved. We had neither the interest in their day-to-day lives and family situations, nor the time to record personal information contained in the messages. They were placed in 'burn bags' and destroyed.

I felt that it was morally justifiable to read these messages in order to do my job properly. It was unavoidable.

Eventually, I learned how to break intercepted messages using working aids.That was the closest I got to the world of Cryptography.[8]

In the late 1950s, the Soviet's main goal was to elicit reaction to their flights by the U.S./Canadian Distant Early Warning Systems and to obtain information on the locations, patrol zones and reaction time of the fighter aircraft deployed against them.

As a Junior Analyst Trainee without a University degree, I would pass my work to my superior and occasionally, with a little polish, it would work its way up the ladder to Senior Analysts who were almost always University graduates.

In 1959, our family moved into a brand new home, a Campeau-built bungalow in the west end of Ottawa. My paternal grandmother and my uncle moved into a house next door. During the past year I had my first experience with fatherhood. I adored my little girl and enjoyed every spare moment I had with her.

In the 1960s, many CSE - then the Communications Branch, National Research Council- employees in the clerical classifications were disgruntled. Much of it had to do with the difference between the CR (Clerical and Regulatory Staff) and the CO (Communications Officers) and the work ethics.

The reclassification of many CR positions to the CO level in the early 1970s improved the attitudes and working relationships, promising non-graduates with special skills an opportunity to move up the ladder to supervisory and management positions.

---

8   Alan Turing; In April 2012, GCHQ released two papers by Alan Turing on the theory of code-breaking. Considered the father of modern computer science, Turing and his brilliant team at Bletchley Park cracked the German ENIGMA system.

FOUR

Because I was active in sports, I soon learned that CBNRC employees were involved in many activities outside of work. We had golf tournaments, a bowling league and basketball, softball, touch football and broomball teams.

For the uninitiated, Broomball is a game originated in Canada played on a regular indoor or outdoor hockey rink by six-man players including a goaltender.

The original broomball sticks were wooden shafts made from household 'corn' brooms. We cut off the bottom half of the brooms and wrapped the remaining hard portion in electrical tape to simulate a hockey stick. Eventually, the corn brooms were replaced by specially-designed aluminum sticks with rubber triangular ends. Players use rubber-soled shoes instead of skates and the ice was smooth and hard to improve traction.

We had three teams in our in-house Broomball League: one from Production Staff, one from the Communications Centre and another from the Technical Staff. We played at the City of Ottawa outdoor hockey rinks in the evenings.

One night, it was blisteringly cold. When you exhaled, you could virtually see your breath hanging in front of you. The running shoes we wore didn't give us any traction and weren't thick enough to keep our feet from freezing. The corn broom sticks were frozen solid.

The wooden skating rink huts had wood-burning stoves so when we changed lines we could run inside and keep warm. It was hilarious. Often, your replacement didn't want to leave the comfortable confines of the huts and return to the ice.

We also entered teams in the National Research Council Bowling tournaments. For years, both of our men and women's teams beat all of the other teams from other NRC Departments.

Of course, they were aware that we were involved in something 'hush-hush' and became frustrated when we wouldn't talk about what we did 'in that building'.

One night, after one of the tournaments we were sitting around at a bar and I decided to have a little fun with them.

"Do you know what we do in our building?

I got their undivided attention.

"We test bowling balls!"

Our Annual Fishing Derby, at White Lake near Arnprior, Ontario in late spring brought the staff and senior management together. Our Chief, Ed Drake was a regular participant and mixed with the rest of the staff – 'one of the guys'. Above all, there was an excellent rapport between the junior members and the executives of CBNRC.

One morning two friends and I arrived at 4 a.m. and found that four people were still playing poker. We offered to make breakfast before everyone went fishing. In those days, it was not surprising to see a case of beer at one end of the boat. Today, that could get you arrested!

In the early 1960s and 1970s, CBNRC employees continued to do well in outside sports. Our bowling teams won most of the NRC tournaments until CBNRC was removed from the NRC umbrella.

Our softball team, bolstered by an integrated U.S. officer who was a great pitcher, and our Touch Football and Basketball teams performed well in the Federal Government Recreation Association League.

The fenced area behind our building was big enough for a group of us to play touch football during lunch hours. Some of the guys who wore their good suits to work - yes, we wore suits in those days- would remove their ties and jackets.

On one occasion, a good friend of mine got too close to the chain-link fence and caught his pants cuff on the sharp edge of one of the bottom links. It ripped his pants all the way up to the crotch. He finished work that day sitting behind his desk, not moving until he left for home walkng carefully to his car.

One day, at lunch hour, two ex-RCMP employees and I were sitting on a bench against the fence inside our compound when a group of children walked by.

One of them pointed and said, "What are those people doing in there?"

Another replied, "I think it's an old man's home!"

20

When we celebrated special events (retirements, promotions, weddings, et al), we held them at the Bytown Naval 'Mess' in downtown Ottawa. There were a couple of rooms available to handle large groups. In another area there was a large bar where active and retired naval personnel and their guests could meet in a pleasant atmosphere complete with piped-in music.

A friend of mine, an-ex Canadian Naval Officer and I attended one of the parties at the Mess one night. He was a real 'maucho' type, a bit laconic but likeable; a true dyed-in-the-wool New York Yankees fan.

While he sat at the bar, I mingled with the CSE staff. I decided to have a beer and headed for the bar. When I got there, I could see my friend at the other end in an animated discussion with another Navy officer.

While I waited for my beer, someone tapped me on the shoulder and said, "Would you like to dance?"

When I turned to face the person, I became apoplectic and I could feel my throat drying up. I stared into this guy's face. I was shocked. It was the first time that any man had asked me to dance. I had heard about these incidents but never before experienced one. As my brain was fumbling around to form a polite response, I noticed my friend at the other end of the bar. He was always playing jokes on me. I owed him one!

"Look, I don't dance but my friend there in the blue suit sitting at the end of the bar loves to dance. I'm sure he would love to dance with you."

The young man smiled, "Thanks, you're a pal." Then he turned and headed towards the other end of the bar.

I breathed a sigh of relief as I gulped down some beer, my eyes trained on the young man. I could see my friend's face as he flushed and his eyes grew large. His head turned and he glared at me. I raised my beer glass in a mock salute to him.

A few moments later, the young man turned and walked away. I never heard the end of it; my friend used some of the language that gnarly seamen choose when aggravated. But, on a number of occasions when we gathered with other friends, he often related the story with his own special sense of humour.

Some may feel that revealing the fact that CSE employees suffered from behavioural problems shed a poor light on the organization. Every organization has at one time or another been confronted by personnel difficulties.

Between 1958 and 1961, we were faced with the pressure of working in a climate of fear about a looming nuclear war involving the Soviets and the U.S. over the Cuban Crisis.

Things were tightened up within the intelligence community. We were constantly under pressure not to speak about our work when outside of CSE and to be cognizant of the level of clearances of the people with whom we worked. Many of us confessed to each other the fear of accidentally saying something which would reveal the mere existence and, heaven forbid, the role of CSE in the intelligence world.

You had to be there, in that pressure-cooker environment, to experience those conditions, to understand how and why we could find some respite in our day-to-day work. Many of us found some relief in the way of quirky humour and 'goofy' things.

Our environment at times created these conditions. When we had a bad day and came home to our families we couldn't talk about our problems or release our tensions which often created an unpleasant atmosphere.

But, at work we became a close knit group, supporting each other and discussing our problems when 'uncleared personnel' weren't around. Most of all, we understood when others became ill because of work-related problems.

We had the same kind of camaraderie when we represented CSE in sports tournaments such as baseball, basketball, bowling, broomball, touch football and golf.

I was very fortunate to have made good friends with three of my co-workers and their wives. We never talked 'shop'. At the office we had to restrict our conversations to those areas in which we were all cleared and we respected that situation without question. The diversity of our areas of expertise meant that some aspects of our work required special clearances only on a need-to-know basis. The first rule was always to protect the source and content of classified material.

FIVE

In June 1961, CBNRC moved to a new building on Riverside Drive and Heron Road, the Sir Leonard Tilley Building. (see images 3 and 4).

What a change that was. Everything was new and we had a lot more space. The view from the building was wonderful. We were close to picturesque 'Hog's Back' and the parkways along the Rideau Canal which is well known in winter to be the World's Longest Skating Rink.

We were very fortunate to have an Exercise Centre for Government employees in a building across the street from the Tilley Building adjacent to the Federal Post Office Headquarters. At lunch hour we could jog indoors around a small track and use the weights. When the weather was good, I used to jog about six kilometers along the paved paths to Carleton University and back. In the winter, I also frequented nearby indoor swimming pools.

That same month, we learned about the defection of two prominent U.S. National Security Agency employees, mathematicians William Martin and Bernon Mitchell, who turned up in Moscow and defected to the Soviets. It was a major shock for the intelligence community.

Security at NSA was tightened up and polygraphs were added to their background security checks. We were all reminded not to discuss the matter with anyone and also our compliance with the Official Secrets Act.

Though I enjoyed working on the analytical side, I realized that the best jobs, the higher paying positions, were in report-writing and as a supervisor. In the next year, I was able to put some short reports together on Foreign Air Operations in the Arctic and work with the senior reporters to glean any knowledge I could.

I eventually worked my way up to a CR4 Clerk level. I was earning pretty good money for those times, about $5,000 a year.

On 18 October 1963, our second daughter, Wendy Lee was born. We only had a month to rejoice in her arrival; on 22 November, the world went into shock at the news of the assassination of President John F. Kennedy.

Everyone who lived through the period remembers where they were when they heard the news of JFK's assassination. Our entire office stood in shock and disbelief in front of a hastily-installed TV set. Walter Cronkite reported: "The U.S. President, John Fitzgerald Kennedy has been shot and is in critical condition in a Dallas hospital". And later with tears in his eyes, he reported the death of the President of the United States.

That year, an event outside of CSE was about to have a profound effect on my life. One day after a round of golf, a CSE pal of mine told me about his part-time job working for the City of Ottawa's Parks and Recreation Department.

As the Director at the Dovercourt Community Centre on Cole Avenue in Westboro, in the west end of Ottawa, he was looking for an assistant Director who would be responsible for a variety of programs targeted to every age group in that particular community. It covered arts and crafts, ballet, table tennis, checkers and sewing on Friday nights and Saturday mornings; and a teenage dance every Friday night. On Wednesday night, they used a local public school for floor games and basketball. I applied and was accepted.

In my first year, I had a golden opportunity to demonstrate that I could handle difficult situations. The Rec and Parks Department sent me to another centre across town where the former Director was having a difficult time with the teenage group.

After two nights, I figured out what the problems were. In one case, merely understanding the age group and actually being interested in what they had to say was the answer. I quickly learned that some parents dropped off their kids for two hours to free them up to shop or visit friends, like a free babysitting service.

The other problem was very simple. All I had to do was replace a light bulb in a dark area of the gymnasium where couples were 'necking'. That may sound very petty in today's world, but in those days parents were shocked when they 'just happened to drop in' to see what was going on!

The following year, my friend retired and I replaced him as Director of the Dovercourt Community Centre. One Friday night, an incident occurred which tested both my instincts and decision-making skills. A 12-year old boy who had come to the dance became violently ill that night. I was advised by a few teenagers that he was sick and vomiting in the Men's Room.

I noticed that his face was very pale and I could smell liquor on his breath. It was actually wine. He had taken a bottle from home and smuggled it into the dance. Unfortunately, he had miscalculated how much his system could withstand.

Now, I know that most adults would have been shocked in the 1960s, but I had been exposed to many children who appeared to be looking for attention when they came to the Centre. I took the boy into my office and phoned his parents only to find that they weren't home.

I realized that I couldn't allow him to leave and I was the only adult at the Centre. So, I called the police. I knew that if he left and injured himself, or became involved in an accident, I would be held responsible.

When the Police Officers arrived, I became very unpopular with the teens that were there. I heard later, in a letter from the Ottawa Recreation and Parks Department, the boy's parents had called to thank me for the way I handled the situation.

That first year was unforgettable. 'Rock and Roll' was growing by leaps and bounds. Our Friday night dances were jammed with teens wanting to hear the latest hits by all the top groups of the day. I was asked to pick up a 45 rpm 'vinyl' record of the Beatles hit 'Roll over Beethoven'. This group and their music was totally unknown to me. Because I usually screened the records I bought, visiting other school and church dances introduced me to this 'new wave' of music geared to teenagers.

I discovered that we had some very impressive local bands, with interesting names: the Rascals, The Staccatos (who became the Five Man Electrical Band) and the Townsmen who later had a superb hit - 'The Lion Sleeps Tonight' I got to know the band leaders and their fellow artists and didn't realize that it would have a significant effect on my life outside the intelligence community.

In November 1964, I was scheduled to visit the Canadian Forces Base (CFB) Alert, Nunavut, on the northeastern tip of Ellesmere Island, Northwest Territories where we had a listening post. The Signals Intelligence (SIGINT) station, manned by Canadian Forces personnel, was tasked with intercepting Soviet radio signals.

(In 1958, while I was waiting to hear from CSE about my appointment, two of my friends were selected to go to Alert. They were joined by Canadian Forces Supplementary Radio System (CFSRS) personnel from the Leitrim Base outside of Ottawa to establish a Signals Intelligence Collection Base. In its formative years, Alert was a 'hardship posting' and the personnel had to endure some difficult situations in that barren land. There was a time when supplies ran pretty low and 'they ate mostly potatoes and powdered food'.)

The site is strategically important because of its proximity to the Soviet Union.[9] Alert is closer to Moscow than it is to Ottawa and it's the closest point in North America to many Russian military installations. These bases gave the Soviets 'first strike capability' against North America.

The trip north was quite an adventure and full of surprises. I flew out of Trenton Air Force Base (AFB) on a C-130 Transport and arrived at Namao AFB in Edmonton, Alberta. They billeted me in military quarters at the base to await my early morning flight to Resolute Bay, Thule, Greenland and CFB Alert.

That night I wandered into the Namao Base recreation hall and watched a few men playing pool. One of the guys with a heavy beard looked very familiar. I walked over to him and said, "You are the spitting image of an Ottawa Radio Announcer at CFRA called General Grant."

He turned to me, stuck out his hand and said, "Hi, I am General Grant, nice to meet you!"

My jaw dropped as he shook my hand and I sheepishly replied, "I'm Ron Lawruk. You gotta be kidding! What are you doing here?"

We all laughed and discussed the extremely cold weather. Grant was part of an entourage visiting the Northern Canadian military bases to entertain the troops before Christmas.

The next morning, I got up at 4 a.m. and hustled out to the tarmac to board the American-made Fairchild C-119 'Flying Boxcar' transport aircraft. I was astonished at the size and age of the aircraft used by the Canadian Armed Forces to resupply the Arctic bases.

I was soon disappointed when informed that the flight was postponed. The flight was re-scheduled until the following day.

I was back in my quarters by 5:30 a.m. and had an entire day to spend in Edmonton, which was quite a distance from the airport. I took a bus downtown and walked around the city. With its winter mantle and a bitterly cold wind, I wasn't impressed.

The next morning I arrived at the transport aircraft and boarded. Inside, there no regular seats, only webbed ones along the hull- the kind that you see in movies where the 'parachute troops' sat.

9   CFS Alert, Wikipedia.org

In the middle were three very large aluminum containers called 'Paul Bunyans' in which supplies were stored.

Fifteen minutes after takeoff, the CF-119 encountered a heater problem near Fort McMurray and we were forced to return to Namao. The flight was again postponed-back to my quarters-with another day to waste in Edmonton. I went into town for dinner and enjoyed the James Bond movie "Goldfinger". I've been a Bond movie fan ever since.

The following morning we took off and finally headed for Alert. Along the way, chains around the Paul Bunyans 'clanged' incessantly. Sleep was impossible because the noise was deafening.

There was one other passenger on the plane. An Inuit woman whom I learned had recovered from TB in an Edmonton hospital was returning to her home in Frobisher Bay.

Frobisher was interesting. I got a good look at the underground tunnels leading to the various buildings.

An hour later we flew north and I was alone in the whole cargo area. When we flew over the fiords of Greenland, I stared out the rear cargo window and saw the tops of the enormous icebergs moving slowly through the Davis Strait. What a sight! It was a barren, white, wild and foreboding world. I wouldn't want to go down in that area.

The American Base at Thule was something to behold in that white wilderness. As we approached, in the extreme darkness of a Northern Arctic night, we saw bright lights on the horizon. It looked like Las Vegas. It was the lights surrounding the airport.

We landed smoothly, disembarked and jumped into covered track vehicles.

Since we were staying overnight, they took me to the PX to register. It was mind-boggling. Here in the frozen north, thousands of miles from civilization, was the most lavishly decorated, furnished nightclub.

As I approached the desk, I couldn't help but notice two people standing at the registration desk. One of them had a great figure with flowing blond hair. I went out of my way to get a good look at this attractive looking chick. When she turned around, I got a real shock.

She-was a he! After all, it was the 60s and 'the times they were a changing'. He was the lead singer in a rock group that would be entertaining the U.S. troops stationed there.

The next morning, at breakfast, I learned that Denmark which owned Greenland allowed the U.S. to operate a staging base to counter

Soviet incursions and/or potential attacks over the Pole. The Danes operated all of the other services on and around the base.

We flew to Alert the following morning. I had finally reached the most northerly inhabited location in Canada which has no sunshine from October to early March.

What a stark and scary sight. It was absolutely white everywhere. Snow was blowing across the runway and one could barely see the track on which we were supposed to land. I could see the outline of the Arctic Ocean where it met the snowy shore.

I have a lot of respect for the pilots who had to operate in this barren land and even more for the crews and the CF-119.

The landing was surprisingly smooth. We were met by a tracked vehicle which transported me to the Officers quarters.[10]

After a briefing by the C.O., a Naval Commander, I was given a tour of the complex. The Headquarters and Operations buildings and the 24 hour dining hall were located in close proximity to the living quarters. Surprisingly, there was a curling rink with one sheet of ice. I had a brief visit with the staff on the First Watch then went to my room before catching the next two shifts.

After a good night's sleep (I couldn't tell the difference between night and day-it was dark all the time), I headed to the Mess for breakfast. You could order anything you wanted day or night; a full breakfast with steak and eggs was one of the most popular dishes. There wasn't much to do when you were off duty, but they fed you very well.

During my tour of the base, I realized that living conditions were rough. Because of the complete darkness and the high winds, blowing snow and frequent 'white-outs', strong thick ropes were strung between each building. One had to hold onto secured safety ropes at all times. It was very easy to become disoriented in that environment. A mistake in that region was life-threatening.

All of the toilets were installed in wooden structures with large holes below the toilet seat, the kind used on many farms in the past. Below the hole was a forty-five gallon empty oil drum, aptly called a 'Honey Bucket'. It had to be removed manually and emptied in an area beyond the settlement.

---

10   CSE staff visiting intercept stations were billeted as Officers

My escort told me that during the freezing days in winter, the Honey Buckets were next to impossible to remove. On a number of occasions, the barrels tipped and the contents spilled onto the clean-up crew. I tried not to visualize the event.

While touring the facilities, I had also noticed a couple of pure white huskies sitting alongside one of the buildings on which a large sign bore the words 'IGLOO GARDENS'.

On the second night of my visit I left the Operations Building and headed for the Mess. As I pulled myself along the ropes, I felt something nudging my hand. I looked down at one of the Huskies and petted its soft fur until I reached the entrance. A private had just closed the door and saw me.

"Wha..what are you doing, sir?" he stammered.

"Going in for dinner. How's the grub?"

"F..Fine. Do you know that's a wolf that you're petting?"

The words struck me as if someone had hammered me with a shovel. I pulled back my hand, counted my fingers and shoved my hand in my pocket. I felt myself lurching for the door. The 'dog' just stared at me with those amazing intense wolf eyes.

"She visits the huskies every night", he explained. "Kind of tame but you never know."

I couldn't get into the building fast enough. Later, I learned that they repeated the story of the CSE guy who petted the wolf. I heard it several times during my career.

I also noticed the reference to 'Ladies Served Free' on the sign outside the Mess. The Base was comprised only of servicemen. (Until 1979, only men were posted to CFS Alert which was under the command of the Canadian Army. That changed in 1980 when DND began posting women to the Arctic Base. Most of the postings lasted six months.)

We discussed CSE's assigned tasking for the station (Classified). I found the exchanges with the intercept operators very useful. I understood their problems firsthand and briefed them on the targets we had assigned. They seemed pleased to speak to someone who received the information that they had collected and could give them some insight into the entire operation-from the collection process through to our final reports.

I could sense their increased enthusiasm when I informed them how important their work was to me as an analyst/reporter. They were very keen to hear how it was used by the intelligence community.

I also learned how bored and lonely that life at an Arctic base could be. Alert was a hardship posting. For many, it was a dismal assignment unless you enjoyed reading, watching old CBC-TV programs on tapes, playing cards and curling.

One day, I visited the curling rink to watch one of the games. It was a lot colder than the rinks back in Ottawa. I knew that after a competitive game of curling it was natural for the curlers to celebrate their wins or 'drown their sorrows' at the Club's bar.

I was also presented with an honorary diploma by one of the Alert Officers which read: 'Ancient and Honourable Order of SHWAILETS' (see image 5) which: "entitles the recipient of endlessly and excessively boasting of having served at this --The Most Northerly Permanently Inhabited Settlement in the World -signed and sealed on this 9th day in November 1964".

The word SHWAILETS stood for 'Shit/Water/Oil/Etcetera'.

On the return flight home, we stopped at Resolute Bay for a Customs and Duty inspection by the Resident RCMP Officer. Late that night we reached Namao Air Force Base. I flew to Trenton Air Base the next day and caught a Canadian Forces bus back to Ottawa.

(In 1997, Signals Intelligence was intercepted remotely using equipment and facilities at Alert, resulting in a drastic reduction in personnel.[11] In April 2009, the Royal Canadian Air Force took command of CFS Alert.)

---

11   National Defence and the Canadian Armed Forces, CFS Alert, 4/11/2013

3. Sir Leonard Tilley Building

4. Tilley Plaque

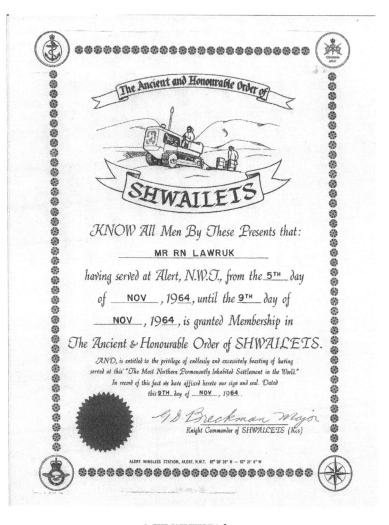

5. SHWAILETS Diploma

SIX

In the spring of 1965, the Director of Recreation for the City of Ottawa asked me to extend my Community Centre duties to take over a new Saturday Evening Night Club for young people between the ages of sixteen and twenty-one. It would be held at Lakeside Gardens in Britannia Park in the west end of Ottawa.

'Lakeside' held many memories for me. In my late teens, I had often taken dates there to dance to the 'Big Band Sounds' of the 1940s and 1950s. But now, we were witnessing a new wave of music: Rock and Roll with Buddy Holly, Chubby Checker, the Beach Boys, the 'King'- Elvis Presley; and the British Sound featuring the Beatles, the Hollies, Dave Clark Five, Petula Clark, the Rolling Stones, and many more.

I was honoured when asked to head up this new program, but I was reluctant to give up another evening, especially every Saturday night. Because they needed a female assistant to monitor the Ladies Wash Room, I was able to convince my wife Jacqueline to take the position. The extra money we would earn would certainly help with our finances.

I was also able to convince the Parks & Recreation Coordinator to hire my Security Guard at the Dovercourt Community Centre to handle any 'rowdies'. The Coordinator gave me full reins and supported me in almost any suggestion I made to create a unique atmosphere for teenagers. Together we developed the idea of a night club and decided to call it 'The Establishment'.

The Coordinator also set up a publicity program and advertised the opening on local radio and television networks. One of the local TV stations had just begun a new dance show called 'Saturday Date' hosted by none other than Peter Jennings, who later became a famous news personality on the ABC network on U.S. Television. He was eventually replaced as host of the dance show by Dick Maloney, a friend of our family.

We set up the hall like a nightclub. Round tables were arranged around the large hall and in the balcony. We had checkered tablecloths and multi-coloured candles on every table (see image 6).

With the assistance of the Lakeside Theatrical Group, we always decorated the stage and displayed photographs of the current group and upcoming attractions. Our budget was set at about $300 for the bands, but some of the rates for the more popular groups were much higher. We tried to keep the price down to an affordable level for that age group.

Opening night was exciting. We didn't know what to expect. After all, we were asking these teenagers who had embraced blue jeans with a vengeance to come to a dance (singles and couples) in their good clothes - no jeans - and to wear a jacket and tie!

To help them, I brought some of my own ties from home for those who forgot, those who weren't aware of the dress code and those who thought they could talk their way in. Jackets could be removed in the dance hall but not the ties. We held fast to the rules with no exceptions and were pleasantly surprised.

Considering the times, we hired a DJ and two eighteen year old 'Go-Go Girls'. Our first musical group was called Thee Groupe headed by Ken Lauzon, son of a local music store owner. (see Image 7). The first song they played was the Beatle hit 'Ticket to Ride'.

As our reputation grew, we brought in the most popular groups like the Staccatos and The Townsmen. On those nights we were sold out a few minutes after the doors opened.

Eventually, we decided to drop the Disc Jockey. I took over the Emcee duties (see Image 8) and introduced the Go-Go Girls and the Bands. One night we played a trick on the crowd by bringing out two nine-year-olds (one was my daughter Debbie) dressed like Go-Go Girls.

Within weeks, we were visited by film crews from both the CBC English and French networks that showed excerpts taken during the evening. I was interviewed by a reporter from The Ottawa Citizen; a full page spread appeared the next day. I was also interviewed on CFRA radio by the well-known local announcer General Grant whom I had met earlier in Edmonton.

At the peak of our popularity, we had major groups from Pittsburg, a vocal trio featuring three beautiful, talented singers called "The Willows" from a Toronto CBC-TV show (see images 9 and 10). and a band from Montreal called The Scepters with a lead singer who sounded like the popular U.S. group, Jay and the Americans.

The success of 'The Establishment' elicited a visit by the Mayor of Ottawa, Don Reid, and his wife on 9 October 1965 who danced and gave their endorsement to the program. A week later, I received a letter from the Deputy Commissioner of Recreation and Parks for the City of Ottawa (see image 11) congratulating us on behalf of the Mayor:

"Please extend my appreciation to everyone involved with the operation of this programme. His Worship was sincerely impressed and pleased with it. Moreover, he told the young people present that he wanted to see the programme expanded.

I was extremely proud of the Department that evening and I want all staff members concerned to know how much the Commissioner and I appreciate their efforts".

Even the Prime Minister of Canada, Lester B. Pearson, was aware of our existence. One night, I introduced a group of young people from his riding in Algoma, Ontario. They were in town for a Liberal Party convention. A few days later, I received a letter (see image 12) dated 26 April 1966 signed by Canadian Prime Minister Pearson:

"May I express to you my sincere appreciation of the very warm reception which you accorded the nine award students from Algoma East on Saturday evening.The students spent a most enjoyable evening at 'The Establishment' at Lakeside Gardens, and were greatly impressed by your kind hospitality and personal attention. Indeed their visit to Ottawa ended on a very happy note".

Because of these endorsements, we had no trouble getting permission to bring in top acts from across Canada and the U.S.

On a few nights, I sat in the balcony and listened to the bands and watched the happy, smiling faces of the young people. As I stood there in a euphoric state, I felt numb with excitement and pride at what I had helped to create. How lucky I was to be part of it. I saw the '60s through eyes that very few parents understood or liked!

Early in 1967, the City of Ottawa decided to completely renovate Lakeside Gardens. We would be forced to move the dance club to another site for approximately one year. We scoured the city for a new hall but were unable to come up with an affordable and suitable location.

Sadly I knew that once we closed the place, it would be difficult to re-capture the atmosphere we had created at Lakeside Gardens.

Meanwhile, a development at CSE would open the door for another event which would significantly change my life. I appreciated the opportunity to work with young people and adults where I could develop my inter-personal skills and become more confident.

Often in life when one door closes another one opens and I was about to prove this saying to be true.

6. Lakeside Gardens, 'The Establishment'

7. THEE GROUPE, Opening Night

8. Ron Lawruk, Director, 'The Establishment'

9. Ron and "The Willows"

10. The Willows in Concert

**DEPARTMENT OF RECREATION
AND PARKS**

214 Hopewell Avenue
Ottawa 1, Ontario
237-5100

ADDRESS ALL CORRESPONDENCE T
COMMISSIONER OF RECREATION AND PA

Your File ....

Our File ....

CORPORATION OF THE
CITY OF OTTAWA
CANADA

March 26th, 1968.

TO WHOM IT MAY CONCERN:

This is to certify that the bearer of this letter,
Mr. Ronald N. Lawruk, has been a part-time employee of the
Department of Recreation and Parks from 1962 to 1968.

During this period Mr. Lawruk has served both as a
seasonal recreation director and as director of our Municipal
Youth Dance Programme, "The Establishment", which operates on
a year round basis.

In his role as recreation director, he was responsible
for the operation of a programme that would appeal to all ages
and interests in a large well established community. Of the
numerous talents displayed by Mr. Lawruk, his obvious ability
to understand and communicate with young people made his appointment to a Municipal Youth Programme a most natural one. The
success of "The Establishment" programme is a direct result of
Mr. Lawruk's enthusiasm and imaginative leadership.

It is our sincere hope that he will return in the near
future to again serve the citizens of Ottawa.

Yours very truly,

(Mrs.) Margaret Farr,
Commissioner.

MF/pv

11. Letter from Ottawa Parks and Recreation Dept

PRIME MINISTER · PREMIER MINISTRE

O t t a w a (4)
26th April, 1966

Dear Mr. Larocque:

May I express to you my
sincere appreciation of the very
warm reception which you accorded
the 9 award students from Algoma
East on Saturday evening.

The students spent a most
enjoyable evening at "The Establishment" at Lakeside Gardens, and were
greatly impressed by your kind hospitality and personal attention.
Indeed their visit to Ottawa ended on
a very happy note.

Please accept my grateful
thanks.

Yours sincerely,

Mr. R. N. Larocque,
Director,
"The Establishment",
1684 Cannon Crescent,
O t t a w a.

12. Letter from Canadian Prime Minister Lester B. Pearson

SEVEN

1967 was a most important year in my life. We traded in our 1964 Ford for a new 1967 bright red VW Beatle. We all loved that little car and it was so economical. That year, our family visited Montreal to see the World Expo.

In the fall of 1967, I applied for and was interviewed for the position as Assistant Liaison Officer to the CSE Canadian Liaison Officer (CANSLO/W) in Washington, D.C. It was a three year posting to the U.S. National Security Agency (NSA) at Fort George G. Meade in Laurel, Maryland beginning in August 1968.

At that time the position was a real plum, only one person was chosen every three years. I estimated that over a thirty year period only ten members of the then - Production staff in CSE would be appointed to the position of Assistant to CANSLO/W.

A few weeks later, I was advised by the Coordinator of Production at CSE that I had been selected. I was delighted.

When I got home, I found that my wife and children didn't have quite the same enthusiasm. Even though we had discussed the possibility and agreed that my career was at a turning point and it could be a pivotal time for me, it was a big sacrifice for them as well.

I could understand their reaction. We were leaving family and friends and going to a new home, a new environment, a new country. For my two daughters, ages five and ten, it meant loss of schoolmates, friends and a new school.

I felt that at thirty-four years of age I was maturing, willing to take a few risks to further my career, to get out and meet new people and to travel. Taking the posting in Washington offered me an avenue into a senior supervisory position - something hitherto only available to University graduates.

Also, at that time, the Canadian dollar was worth about $1.08 U.S. I would be paid in Canadian dollars and my rent would be subsidized. Most of the CSE staff would have killed to get that posting.

We had to rent our house on Cannon Crescent in the west end of Ottawa and hunt for a home in Maryland. The first part was easy. A fellow CSE employee had been looking for a place and had no children, so we rented it to him for the three years.

In March 1968, while we were preparing to fly to Washington to look for a rental house, we were shocked to learn that Martin Luther King had been assassinated. We were more than concerned and apprehensive about the move to the U.S. Capital. Race riots in black communities in Washington shown on TV exacerbated the situation. My wife was afraid to go and I had my doubts as to our safety. We finally overcame our fears and decided to go.

Our flight to Baltimore Friendship Airport was scheduled for the first week of April. We were met by my new boss, CANSLO/W, and we headed towards D.C. He drove us through the city past the Lincoln and Jefferson Memorials and around the Ellipse.

It was a harrowing experience. We arrived during a demonstration by 100,000 people for Martin Luther King. It was scary, driving around Washington through those enormous crowds. My wife and I felt uneasy as the vehicle moved through and around the thousands of people in the central area of the Capital. Our hotel in Silver Springs, Maryland had a much more relaxing atmosphere.

With the assistance of my predecessor, we found a home in Silver Springs, in the Kemp Mill Estates not far from Wheaton. I would have a twenty-two mile drive to NSA in Laurel, Maryland and a ten mile drive to the Canadian Embassy in downtown Washington.

After signing the rental agreement, we registered the two girls in their respective schools which were a couple of blocks from our house. Two days later, we flew back to Ottawa.

In late April, my wife and I attended a Liberal Party rally for Pierre Elliot Trudeau in Hull, Quebec across the Ottawa River. Trudeau was expected to be the new leader of the Party and eventually became Prime Minister while we were in Washington.

On 6 June, while we were finalizing preparations for our move, Bobby Kennedy was murdered. It was all over the news. Our family was shocked and it again raised doubts about our decision to move to Washington. Our friends were surprised that we would leave the safety of Canada for the U.S., especially Washington where the riots and demonstrations were visually portrayed on all of the U.S. and Canadian TV news channels.

In late July 1968, we watched the moving van pull away from our home carrying our household goods. The next day, we piled into our 1967 VW and headed for Washington. We took two days to get there, stopping at Allentown, Pennsylvania to let the girls relax and swim at the motel.

It was blistering hot the whole month of August when I drove through the Maryland countryside to the National Security Agency at Fort George G. Meade, near the city of Laurel. Apparently, the Agency site was chosen because of its distance away from Washington, in case of a nuclear attack.

I was astounded by the size of the complex surrounded by two high chain link wire fences. I also noticed that there was no sign at the entrance to indicate which government department was using the building. (Apparently, a sign was placed in the Main entrance in the 1990s).

Marine guards were posted at every entrance and one needed proper ID just to get into the reception area.

I was allotted a private parking spot in the first row, right in front of the entrance - one of the perks! My predecessor escorted me to our office on the eighth floor of the Headquarters Building where I was greeted by the Senior Liaison Officer (CANSLO/W) and his secretary both of whom I had previously met in Ottawa.

I had my own office adjacent to CANSLO/W with a marvelous view of the Maryland countryside. The following day, CANSLO/W escorted me to the ninth floor of the building to meet the NSA Director, General Marshall Carter and his support staff with whom I would work very closely.

During the next week, my predecessor reviewed my duties and escorted me around the enormous complex, introducing me to contacts in various departments. A few weeks later, my wife and I were privileged to have been invited to a dinner party at the General's home.

In order to fulfill the requirements levied by the Canadian Ambassador to Washington and his staff we had to be cognizant of political activities and international developments involving other countries in the world.

I was responsible for liaising with NSA staff on behalf of CSE involving intelligence collection and reporting, technical exchanges, and visits by officers to/from both organizations. I will never forget the comment of one of their staff that I met on my first day at NSA. He told me that NSA meant 'Never Say Anything'. Another version was: 'No Such Agency'.

We also had to provide clearances for visits by Canadian Officers to other U.S. intelligence agencies including the Pentagon, Central Intelligence Agency (CIA), Defence Intelligence Agency, U.S. Navy/Air Force and Army institutions, military bases and training centers.

After the departure of my predecessor, I also assumed responsibility for furnishing intelligence material to the Canadian Ambassador in Washington.The special material was handled by a Canadian Military Attache at the Embassy. We became good friends. Little did I know that he would unwittingly become an important part of my career at CSE.

The most significant information involved areas in the world where Canadian Peacekeeping Forces had been deployed. The intelligence could reveal facts not available from any other source. It gave me an insight into the reasons for protecting our sources – without this source the free world wouldn't have known the true facts!

Eventually, I got to meet our Canadian Ambassador and his wife who were warm and charming people. It was a special function to which both CANSLO/W and I were invited to attend. The RCMP Commissioner in Washington was returning to Ottawa. Arrangements were made to have fresh lobster flown in from the Maritimes. It was my first taste of lobster and I was hooked.

The first year in Washington was busy and exciting. I found life in the hot summer and fall rather interesting. The humidity was suffocating at times. The temperatures outdoors in July and August reached close to 100 degrees. You left your air-conditioned house and got into your air-conditioned car and drove to your air-conditioned office.

In the month of December, we attended many official and unofficial cocktail parties. Five were related to a one week visit by the Chief of CSE and another Senior Manager. While CANSLO/W escorted the Chief, I escorted the Manager. On one of those nights, my wife and I were included on the guest list at a dinner party at a General's home in Fort Myer, Virginia. It was a luxurious home on the Potomac River and my second exposure to life at this social level.

After introductions, we enjoyed some appetizers with our cocktails. Later, the General invited us to the Dining Room. Each setting at the dinner table had at least four forks, knives and spoons. The general's aide noticed our quizzical looks and leaned over to whisper, "Start from the outside".

From the outset, we were warned about travelling around Washington and Baltimore at night. Since CANSLO/W was an attaché at the Embassy we were invited to a number of official and unofficial functions. One of these proved to be traumatic for CANSLO/W's secretary. She had arranged for her mother, who was visiting her, to go to a party at the Embassy.

That evening, she parked her car near the Embassy and headed for the front door. When they walked past some bushes a man jumped out and grabbed her mother's purse. Her mother had a steel grip on the purse and was knocked to the ground. The assailant dragged her along the cement sidewalk for half a block. I don't remember whether or not she lost the purse.

Her mother suffered scratches and bruises but recovered from the ordeal a short time later. It was a warning to all of us to always be on our guard and to travel in groups, especially at night.

The Canadian Ambassador and his wife were delightful and gracious. This was confirmed on other social visits such as the annual Christmas Party. Our eleven year old daughter was surprised and excited when she was invited to act as an elf during that event.

One of our close family friends, a Canadian Army Captain, was also posted to Washington and we had an opportunity to celebrate our first Washington Christmas with him and his wife.

The Prime Minister of Canada, Pierre Elliot Trudeau (see image 13) visited Washington in March 1969. Embassy Staff were invited to meet him at the Canadian Embassy and I had the pleasure of shaking his hand.

He made quite a speech and raised a few eyebrows at the National Press Club in Washington when he said, "Living next to you (the USA) is in some ways like sleeping with an elephant. No matter how friendly and even-tempered the beast, one is affected by every twitch and grunt!" That's me with the dark glasses to the right of the Prime Minister.

One of my main tasks at NSA was to escort visitors to various Departments within the Agency. This gave me an in-depth insight into the diverse activities of NSA and its affiliated military and governmental agencies in the Washington region. I also participated in a Security Awareness Program and received an award. (see image 14). As Assistant to CANSLO/W, I was responsible for the visits of CSE visitors at the Junior Management level. If CANSLO/W was away or ill, I handled the Senior Management visitors.

Entertaining was a different matter. CANSLO/W had a budget. So, when Senior CSE officers visited NSA they were hosted with a party or a dinner on his budget. However, when CSE staff below the Senior Management level visited, nothing formal was done.

Many of these visitors were friends and co-workers. They were holed up in hotel rooms for up to four nights. Although I had no entertainment budget, I often invited them to our home for dinner. On many occasions, when it didn't interfere with my home life, I would also take them on tours along Rock Creek Parkway to the White House, the Washington Monument, the Ellipse, Arlington Cemetery, the Lincoln and Jefferson memorials and all of the other 'sights' in the downtown core area.

13. Meeting Prime Minister Pierre Trudeau, Canadian Embassy in Washington

14. National Security Agency Security Awareness Award

EIGHT

We had a rodent problem with our first home in Silver Springs and decided to move. We found a beautiful home in the same area near the girls' schools.

When our two daughters began to learn U.S. history in school, I decided to take them on car trips to the various Civil War sites like Gettysburg, Manassas and Harper's Ferry, Washington's home in Mount Vernon and the Smithsonian museums. Along the way, we would stop and read all of the roadside plaques on the highways around Washington.

I learned that the majority of our neighbours were Jewish. Our next door neighbour was a dentist; they also had two girls who were attending the same schools. Our families became good friends.

When we discussed our respective occupations, I told him that I was an Assistant Attache at the Canadian Embassy. I never told anyone that I worked at NSA.

On one occasion, an observant neighbour noticed that every morning I headed east instead of south to get to downtown Washington. I told him that I picked up one of the staff who lived a bit east of our subdivision.

Our dentist neighbour subsequently sponsored us for a membership at the Jewish Swimming Pool. We spent many weekends there throughout the steamy summers. I was the only gentile on their water volleyball team and played against other area teams.

Through the Embassy, I managed to get special tours of the FBI and the White House (see image 15) when my parents visited us from Ottawa. My Dad particularly enjoyed the machine gun demo in the FBI's basement firing range. One of the agents gave my daughter the paper target complete with all of the bullet holes.

Being a golfer and working at NSA allowed me to join the Fort Meade Golf Club at a reduced rate. On a couple of occasions I played with

49

my boss, CANSLO/W, after work. I found, however, that the heat and humidity, especially in July and August, was brutal on the golf course.

For the next three years, I played at the Fort Meade course with a great bunch of NSA employees and ex-servicemen with whom I remained in contact long after I returned to Canada. We had sixteen players including a retired Army Colonel. That was significant, because the senior officers could obtain tee off times *before* the regular troops.

In 1969, I experienced my first direct encounter with racial discrimination. One of the members of our golf group also owned a home in Myrtle Beach, South Carolina, a golf Mecca. In the fall of 1969, he and I organized a trip there.

Seven members of our group signed up to go. We needed one more to have two foursomes. I volunteered to arrange for the seven day trip including the hotel. We booked the Chesterfield Inn. The total cost per person was $120. That included six full breakfasts, five dinners and five days of golf. We would drive down in two cars. The Colonel arranged for a golf game at Fort Bragg in North Carolina on our first day.

When I called other players in the group about the arrangements and the cost, a black American, who was a Colonel, told me that he couldn't go.

I asked "Why not?"

He replied: "In South Carolina, I can't share a room or play golf in a group with a white man. If you had four Black Americans, we could share a room and play together, but you are not allowed to mix the races in a hotel or on a golf course in South Carolina."

I was shocked. It was almost the 1970s. I said, "I thought that discrimination was over!"

"Not in South Carolina and a few other States," he replied.

I told him to wait until I called the Chesterfield Inn to confirm what he had told me.

He was correct. The hotel manager confirmed that they had to adhere to the State laws. I was stunned and very angry, but we could do nothing about it.

We had to find another white man, abhorrent as that may sound. We finally convinced one of our other friends to come along.

On the third day of our trip, we played at the Pine Lakes Country Club, one of the oldest and prestigious golf courses in the area. Most of the staff, especially the bag boys and greens-keeping staff were black Americans.

We had two tee-off times. My group was between two foursomes composed of four Black Americans. On one of the short par three holes, we had just finished putting out, when a ball bounced onto the green narrowly missing us.

That's a no-no in golf. You are supposed to wait until the players ahead of you have moved off the green and out of range. We all turned around to glare at the group behind us. Under the circumstances we refrained from making any comments.

However, as we approached the next tee, the four black American players playing ahead of us had finished hitting and were walking off the tee. One of them made a straight line towards us and with a gesture towards the group behind us, said, "Now that's a bunch of n...ers."

In 1969, General Carter was replaced as Director of NSA by Admiral Noel Gayler. We were invited to the Admiral's home for dinner one evening. He and his wife were very gracious hosts. I was surprised to learn that he was the first U.S. Navy pilot to receive *three* Navy Crosses.

The Admiral was Director from 1969 until 1972 when he was appointed to the Commander in Chief of the Pacific Fleet in Hawaii.[12]

As Assistant to CANSLO/W, I was also fortunate to have the opportunity to escort groups to various Agencies within the U.S. One of these involved a 1969 visit to Kelly Air Force Base in San Antonio, Texas. A five-man CSE party had been invited to inspect new technical equipment being used at the U.S. base. I was responsible for recording the details of the meeting for CSE.

We flew out of Andrews Air Force Base on a U.S. military aircraft used by the Commandant of Kelly Air Force Base, who happened to be returning to the base that day. The Presidents aircraft, Air Force One, was parked on one of the ramps.

When the Colonel learned that we were the Canadian team visiting his base for an exchange of information, he invited us to a cocktail party that night. Before we landed in San Antonio, we asked his Aide to present

---

12   Although I had already returned to Canada in 1971, while watching the TV coverage of U.S. P.O.W.'s returning to the Philippines from Vietnam, I was pleasantly surprised. There was Admiral Gayler, accompanied by Philippine President Marcos, greeting the POW's as they stepped off the aircraft. Gayler died in 2011 at the age of 97.

him with a bottle of Gin with our compliments. That night, he introduced us as 'a fine bunch of Canadians'.

We spent three days in San Antonio, Texas (see image 16). On the weekend, we visited the Alamo Mission. I was surprised to learn that in some areas only one to two feet of the original structure remained after the U.S. patriots clashed with Mexican troops commanded by President Santa Anna (see image 17).

On Saturday night, we stood on a downtown corner and watched the wild Texas drivers as they raced at 'breakneck' speeds from one light to the next, screeching their tires and leaving a lot of rubber on the asphalt.

In late 1969, my wife and I decided to take advantage of the tremendous savings in the prices of cars purchased through the Embassy. We bought a brand new 1970 Ford LTD for $4200.

In 1970, because of the expansion of NSA to the Friendship Airport area, CSE decided to add another position to the CANSLO office. The new Deputy CANSLO position was filled by one of my close golfing buddies at CSE. When he arrived, he assumed some of my duties, especially the NSA visits by Senior CSE Managers.

That year we experienced a phenomenon in Washington which occurs once every seventeen years: a Cicada infestation. You could hardly see through the clouds of flying insects but you could hear them crunch under your feet and your car tires. The streets, cars and houses were covered with them. They were harmless but a nuisance.

During my final year at NSA, I recommended to CANSLO/W that I visit each NSA Department responsible for monitoring foreign activities and submit an across-the-board overview to the respective Groups in CSE.[13]

So, in addition to the normal duties of accompanying CSE staff to their appropriate Agency contacts, I visited each of our associated NSA Departments and produced a document on their operations, responsibilities and future projects. I was impressed by NSA's decision to allow their analyst/reporters to provide comments on their reports because "they were best equipped to manage and analyze their own product".

That year, CSE shifted many of their CR Clerk classifications to Communications Officers. My job was designated as a Communications

---

13   James Bamford; 'Body of Secrets, Anatomy of the Ultra Secret National Security Agency' published in 2001

Officer level 2. It made a big difference to me and many of my co-workers at CSE who had been classified as Clerks. To me, it meant recognition for a person who had been able to achieve an Officer position with only a High School Diploma.

The three years in Washington and my exposure to the U.S. Intelligence community was invaluable. I left there with a broad knowledge of the operations of NSA related to the Soviet Union and the Warsaw Pact countries.

The experience provided me with the self-confidence and background to tackle any challenge that came my way in future positions at CSE.

In the spring of 1971, I was informed that I would be assigned to a desk responsible for analysis and reporting on Foreign Activities in the Arctic.

15. White House Visit with my Family and Parents, 1969

16. CSE Team Arrival, Kelly AFB, San Antonio, Texas

17. Author at the Alamo

NINE

At CSE, I researched classified and 'open source' articles on Foreign Military, Scientific, Economic and Civil Maritime activities in the Arctic that dated from the early 1930s to 2013. The study comprised 80 to 90 % collateral material.[14] I spent many hours at the library and at home reading several unclassified books and periodicals.

It had been widely known and openly published in scientific circles that the Soviets were establishing research camps on the ice in the Arctic Ocean. I checked for scientists and their organizations, the types of research they conducted, and the potential involvement of and use to the military.

Since 1920, Soviet scientists from major research organizations, chiefly the Arctic and Antarctic Research Institute (AARI) organized hundreds of expeditions into the high Arctic. AARI and AANII, the Arctic and Antarctic Scientific Research Institute, are located in St. Petersburg.

Many Soviet scientists openly published their research findings in unclassified press releases and scientific periodicals.[15] This material identified the locations of the ice camps, the resupply support by transport aircraft and to some extent the type of activities being conducted. The Soviets also used immense ice islands capable of handling larger aircraft, posing a threat to other countries around the Pole.

Soviet high latitude aerial expeditions were made to locations off the northernmost coast of Russia such as Franz Josef Land, Novaya Zemlya

---

14   Wikipedia; Soviet Scientific Operations in the Arctic (various articles)

15   Wikipedia and International Journal of Climatology Volume 16; Locations of Soviet Drifting Ice Stations, 1954-1990; Soviet Arctic and Antarctic Institute (AARI and AANII)

and the Novosibirskiy (New Siberian) Islands. Scientists were also active from Soviet Civilian and Military Research vessels along the Arctic coast. Soviet Antarctic expeditions began in 1958.

The Arctic ice floes and islands moved in an anti-clockwise rotation, affording Soviet, U.S. and Canadian scientists with varying specialties the opportunity to conduct research on a wide variety of disciplines and to take measurements of the topography of the ocean floor, the ridges and the mountains.

Soviet open source reports stated that between 1930 and 1990, thirty-one Soviet North Pole (NP) ice stations were manned. Four of these, NP-6, -18,-19 and -22, were established on ice islands. As of November 2014, the most current station was NP-40.

From these NP stations, various departments within the AARI conducted complex research in the fields of oceanology, oceanography, marine biology, meteorology, glaciology, polar geography, gravimetry, hydrophysics, hydrochemistry and hydrology.

Much of the research from these stations led them to major geographic discoveries and allowed them to identify significant underwater features in the Arctic. Charts were made of the water and ice circulation and the under-ice acoustic environment. Records were made on the impact on acoustics and ambient noises, the formation of polynias (open areas of weaker ice) which would be invaluable for submarine expeditions.

The Soviets were far ahead of the other countries in identifying the topographical features of the Arctic, then claimed and named them.

The Lomonosov Ridge discovered in 1948 stretches from the New Siberian Islands to Ellesmere Island in the Canadian Arctic archipelago. Another significant feature is the Mendeleev Ridge, which stretches from the Siberian Shelf to the central stations of the ocean. The Soviets contend that they are extensions of the Eurasian continent but it has never been accepted by the international scientific community.

I decided to take additional in-house classes to bring my Russian language skills up to a higher level. I also took courses at Carleton University and the University of Ottawa in the evenings to hone my writing skills.

The in-house classes were carried out on the top floor of the Sir Leonard Tilley Building. There were eight CSE personnel on the course. From that room we had a wonderful view of the Vincent Massey Park beyond the Public Works parking lot.

During breaks, we would look out the window and watch the people walking around. On a few occasions, especially Friday afternoons, we noticed a car entering the parking lot around 2:00 p.m. and parking in the same spot a distance from all of the other cars. It remained there for about two hours.

After a while, we became suspicious and informed our Security Officer. I thought that it might be someone trying to pick up electronic signals from our building.[16]

We continued to monitor the automobile's regular trips to the parking lot from our window. One day, we noticed another car following the automobile into the lot but parking a short distance away. It turned out to be an observation car.

We all stood at the window staring down at the two cars as a police car entered the lot and moved quickly towards the suspect vehicle. Suddenly, two other men dashed from the observation car and approached from the rear.

Seconds later, an older man and a young woman exited the car with their hands held high over their head. The officers frisked them then looked inside the vehicle. The Policemen spent about ten minutes questioning the couple before they let them return to their car and leave.

A few days later, I learned that the couple, from nearby Carleton University, were having an affair. One was believed to be a Professor and the other his student. Our excitement over a 'potential threat to CSE's security' was ended.

There were other odd incidents over the years that were reported by some of the staff in other areas of CSE. In one of the offices facing the Post Office HQs building on Heron Road, CSE employees were periodically asked by supervisors to shut the blinds. One of the staff asked, "Is the light bothering you."

They were eventually told that unidentified persons were suspected of conducting surveillance of our building using cameras, telescopes and recording devices. On a couple of occasions the typing pool was not allowed to use the telephones or electric typewriters.

---

16   New York Times, March 26,, 1985; The U.S. discovered devices in electronic typewriters in the U.S. Embassy in Moscow. The equipment allowed the Soviets to simultaneously copy and store what a secretary was typing on an electronic typewriter

Warsaw Pact countries were purported to have perfected a device to actually intercept details entered on electronic typewriters from a mobile site located in a nearby building or a vehicle. There was no evidence to prove that this incident was related.

In 1972, I ran across an old buddy from the Canadian Embassy in Washington. He had returned to NDHQ to work for the Directorate of Scientific and Technical Intelligence (DSTI).

He asked if we could provide him with any available intelligence on a possible Soviet presence on Spitsbergen Island in the Svalbard Archipelago located to the north of Norway.

A week later, I received an official DSTI request outlining their requirements. I delivered a copy of the request to CSE's Coordinator of Production (COORD/P) office.

We were able to provide some information on the subject

In the fall of 1972, many of the CBNRC reporting positions were being evaluated for future upgrading. In my case it was from a Communications Officer (CO) Level 2 to a CO3. At that time my Manager was the CBNRC Union representative in the National Research Council. One of our CO2s, a young woman and I were selected to appear before the Board to decide if our positions were to be re-designated to the CO3 level.

The Manager was instrumental in guiding us in formulating our approach to the special board. His support and guidance afforded all CO2s in CBNRC the opportunity to raise their job classification level.

The members of the board included a CBNRC Senior Manager, the National Research Council Evaluator and a member of the Canadian Federal Government Treasury Board.

During my session, the level of contacts I had within the Department of National Defence was questioned and claimed to be at a lower level. Moreover, the CBNRC representative stated that there was no officiial written requirement on the CSE file associated with the DSTI request.

Luckily, I had prepared some evidence and arguments just in case we were asked. I pulled out my copy of the DSTI memorandum and the note attached to the original which I had passed to the CSE COORD/P's office (complete with date stamp).

The Treasury Board Representative looked over the letter, handed it back to me and said, 'This interview is over'.

A few days later my female co-worker and I were advised that we were being promoted to CO3s. It meant that many of the CO2's in CSE could ask for a re-evaluation. Eventually, a great many of them also received the promotion to CO3's without having to go through a nerve-wracking interview. We felt like trail-blazers. A few years later, it happened again.

In the fall of 1973, I was placed in charge of a staff of four analyst/reporters in another associated department. I was privileged to have such experienced, competent people with which to work.

In January 1974, CSE came under close scrutiny by the Canadian Broadcasting Corporation (CBC)-Television Network program, The Fifth Estate. The program suggested that 'CSE was engaged in Signals Intelligence and that one of its users was the CIA'. Many media representatives stood outside the front gate of the Tilley Building waiting to interview CBNRC staff; they called us 'Spooks'.

Employees had to be re-acquainted with the Official Secrets Act and escorted to and from the building. I remember that one of our female staff members was very nervous and I escorted her right to her car in the parking lot.

TEN

For decades, the Soviet Chief Directorate of the Northern Sea Route[17] openly reported its success in moving merchant vessels laden with supplies through the NSR between the Barents Sea and the Kamchatka Peninsula. In recent years, with the development of Soviet nuclear icebreakers, the Lenin, the nuclear-powered Arktika and the Ermak-classes, the most powerful icebreakers in the world, transits in the NSR were successful.

The icebreakers escorted merchant vessels during resupply runs along the NSR from Murmansk in the west to Soviet communities along the Arctic coast to ports in the Pacific Ocean. Canada was considering development and/or purchase of a nuclear icebreaker to augment or replace our aging fleet led by the icebreaker Louis St Laurent.

In November 1974, I recommended that we approach the Canadian Coast Guard Service (CCGS) to determine if they had any interest in these activities.

I met with the Chief of the CCGS in Ottawa to discuss the subject. The Chief responded that Canada was interested in obtaining a modern icebreaker. He was particularly interested in obtaining details on the capabilities of the new Soviet Arktika-class nuclear-powered icebreaker which was scheduled to begin operations in 1975.

A short time later, he sent an official requirement to CSE. He also recommended that one of my staff and I visit the Louis St. Laurent in the Gulf of St. Lawrence during the coming winter to acquaint ourselves with icebreaking operations.

---

17   Internet, various articles on the Northern Sea Route (Russia); Ukraine Timeline Nuclear Icebreaker Arktika, Arctic Legend: Saving North Pole Conqueror, 9 October 2012

My immediate Supervisor and our Senior Manager approved the visit. I selected a woman analyst on my staff.

In March 1975, we flew to Stephenville, Newfoundland via Halifax, Nova Scotia. The next morning, we went down to the harbour and were picked up by a CCGS helicopter.

The flight over the ice-covered Gulf of St Lawrence was exciting since it was the first time either of us had ever flown in a helicopter. There was little to see but snow and ice until we saw a red vessel on the horizon, the Louis St. Laurent. Considering the near white-out conditions, I could understand why the vessel was painted red. The pilot informed us that due to the tremendous ice pressure, the ship was temporarily locked-in (see image 18).

The heavy turbine electric icebreaker was launched in 1966 and commissioned in 1969. In September 1969, she joined the U.S. icebreaking Tanker SS Manhattan expedition in the Northwest Passage.

After landing on the ship, we were met by the First Officer and escorted below to meet Captain Paul Fournier. The Captain's wife was on board. I assumed that it may have been planned for my co-worker's comfort. It was particularly nice to have other topics of conversation at our evening meals with the Captain and his wife (see image 19).

We spent three days on the vessel. The First Officer gave us a tour of the entire ship. One of the highlights of the trip occurred when we walked to an area inside the hull at the bow of the ship. The sounds of the ice smashing against the hull were so loud that we had to cover our ears.

We were also allowed to climb up to the Crow's Nest (see image 20) to view the ice breaking operation. I got some great photos as the vessel sliced through the ice. It was astounding to watch the three foot thick ice split into chunks as it was hurled left and right of the vessel. Light and dark blue hues were clearly evident on some of the thicker older ice.

On our way back to the port of Sydney, we accepted an invitation by the Captain to observe the ice from their helicopter. We flew over the Gulf, along the coast passing over Peggy's Cove and returned to the icebreaker which was heading for the harbor. That day we bade farewell to the Captain, First Officer and crew and left the Louis St. Laurent.

The following year, the Louis St. Laurent made a partial transit of the Northwest Passage. In 1979, she made a full east to west transit of the

Northwest Passage and circumnavigated North America. She aslso made another historic voyage in 1994.[18]

In April 1975, CBNRC was officially removed from the NRC umbrella and transferred to the Department of National Defence. We became the Communications Security Establishment (CSE).

New Federal government regulations were also instituted for employees in supervisory positions who were required to become bilingual and to attend special French Language classes or lose their jobs.

My mother was French and I sincerely believed that it was good to be able to speak more than one language. Some of my friends were the first to take the three week course. They were aware of the fact that if they couldn't complete the course satisfactorily, they could lose their position and be moved to another job.

When confronted with the fact that after twenty years of service to CSE, a fifty-five year old friend of mine was told that if he didn't become bilingual, he would lose his job. He was raised in England and was never exposed to the French language. He had a mild heart attack and his health was never the same.

I was sent on the course and found it challenging. One of the men in our class, a senior civil servant from Public Works decided that he was not going to cooperate. When he wanted to go to the Men's Room, the instructor told him he had to ask in French. He refused. Eventually, he was asked to leave the class. I don't know what became of him. After three weeks, I completed the course and went back to work.

In April 1975, I visited our Arctic Intercept Station at Inuvik, Northwest Territories. I was the only passenger on board the C130 Hercules aircraft when we flew from Namao Air Force Base in Edmonton to Yellowknife, Northwest Territories (see image 21). Along the way, the pilot invited me to sit in the co-pilot's seat. I put on a headset and listened to the air-to-ground communications between the crew and the air traffic controllers.

---

18   Wikipedia, 22 August 1994, The Louis St. Laurent and the U.S. Coast Guard vessel (USCGC) Polar Sea, with 60 Canadian and U.S. scientists on board, conducted a Joint Scientific Expedition to become the first North American surface vessels to reach the North Pole. There, they met up with the Soviet icebreaker Yamal which was 'carrying a number of tourists'.

Visiting Inuvik when there were twenty-four hours of sunlight was unusual. I woke up one night at 3 a.m., pulled aside the heavy dark blinds and looked out. It was bright and sunny like a July afternoon in Ottawa.

I spent two days at the station talking to operators about our tasking and gave them some insight into CSE's role in monitoring foreign activities in the Arctic.

18. Icebreaker Louis St. Laurent in Gulf of St. Lawrence, 1975

19. Dinner on board the St. Laurent with Captain and his wife

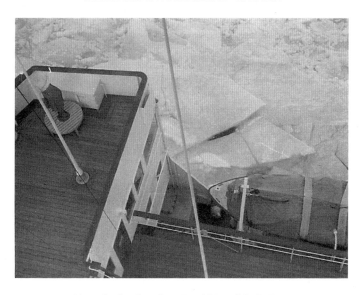

20. View of icebreaking from Crow's Nest of the St. Laurent

21. Enroute to Yellowknife and Inuvik, NWT

ELEVEN

In May 1975, I attended my first conference, the CANUKUS Maritime Intelligence Conference, held at the Congress Centre in Ottawa. Representatives of their respective countries contributed and presented intelligence papers for discussion on Foreign Maritime developments. The Conference included both Naval and Merchant Maritime delegates; the CSE delegation had heretofore never included any members from my area of responsibility.

Although I was only an observer, I managed to meet delegates from various U.S. and U.K. intelligence agencies who were interested in the new Soviet nuclear icebreakers.

There were sessions in which the Russian icebreakers *Lenin* and *Arktika* were mentioned, particularly by one member of the British delegation. I had also been reading articles released by the Soviets on the *Arktika* which we had passed to the Chief of the Canadian Coast Guard.

Nearing the end of the Conference, I decided that it was time that we should become involved in future discussions. I stood up in front of the 200 delegates and observers and proposed that they should consider a CSE Conference Paper for the 1976 Conference in London, England.

"I would like to propose a paper on the development of the Soviet Nuclear Icebreaker Fleet and its potential to advance the Soviet presence in the Arctic and protect its territorial claims".

The Head of the Canadian Delegation from the Directorate of Defence Intelligence (DDI) at NDHQ shot back, "That sounds like a great idea. Are you prepared to write and present such a paper?"

"Yes, I am."

"We will add it to the proposed list for next year's conference and contact CSE at a later date". I sat down with a sense of elation and relief.

The members of my staff were quite surprised that I made the proposal. We were pleased that we would finally be able to provide additional support to the Canadian Coast Guard Service. This boosted both my confidence and the morale of my staff.

We were all very busy working on the conference paper through the fall of 1975. We had to scour through thousands of newspaper, scientific and military books and periodicals for any technical information on these vessels. The paper was completed in February 1976. I submitted it to my boss at CSE and delivered it to DDI in March 1976.

It was traditional for Delegates from CSE to visit British counterparts at Government Communications Headquarters (GCHQ) in Cheltenham the week prior to the Annual CANUKUS Conference for Signals Intelligence discussions and to review the papers being presented. So I was slated to spend a week in Cheltenham and a week in London.

Because a family friend in the Canadian Air Force was stationed in Lahr, Germany, my wife decided to join me after the London conference so we could travel to Europe together. Our two daughters had grown up: Debbie, now 18, was old enough to take care of the house and watch over Wendy, her 13 year old sibling. Both girls had attended St. Daniel's Catholic School in the west end of Ottawa. Debbie had gone on to Laurentian High School where she was a cheerleader. Wendy eventually went to St. Joseph's for grades 7 and 8 where she became Head Girl. She also attended Laurentian and graduated in 1981.

In May 1976, I was in a euphoric state. I was actually going to travel across the Atlantic and visit England, Holland, France, Germany, Switzerland and Italy.

I joined two of my CSE co-workers and a large contingent from DDI, NDHQ at the Ottawa International airport. We boarded a Canadian Services Boeing 727 aircraft on a late night scheduled Canadian military flight to London.

It was my first trip across the pond. Because it was dark, I wasn't sure if we were over land or water. The seats were comfortable but the food left a lot to be desired. I closed my eyes and tried to sleep but the engine and cabin noises were very disruptive.

It seemed as if I had no sooner closed my eyes when the sun came up and it was daylight. Soon everyone was awake and breakfast was being served.

After landing at Gatwick Airport, the DDI staff headed for London and our CSE team took a train to Cheltenham in the Cotswold Mountains. Stone cottages and medieval villages surround the city famous for being one of the locations used to film the Sherlock Holmes movie, The Hound of the Baskerville, complete with fog, moors and mist.

It also has one of the most popular racetracks in England and is the location of GCHQ, the British version of CSE.

I was able to meet my British counterparts and discuss Signals Intelligence items of common interest to both organizations. I found the topics we discussed and the pre-Conference sessions most informative. It gave all of the participants an opportunity to discuss problems pertaining to Soviet and Warsaw Pact targets, analytical and reporting techniques and the papers to be presented at the upcoming Conference.

I was pleased that my paper was given close scrutiny and accepted by everyone present. It gave me a great boost to know that I would have their support at the London conference.

After our meetings in Cheltenham, my two CSE companions and I took the train to London for the CANUKUS Maritime Intelligence Conference. We arrived at the Trafalgar Hotel near Piccadilly Circus the same afternoon. London was a bustling, active and vibrant city with much to offer. It was a major highlight in my life.

The summer of 1976 in England was one of the hottest on record; one day it reached 80 degrees Fahrenheit! It was so hot that I left the door to my hotel room open until I went to bed.

On Saturday morning, I began my sight-seeing tour armed with fresh fruit and a bottle of water purchased from a street stand. A double-decker bus took me a couple of miles away from the hotel. Then, following a London City map, I started to walk back to my hotel.

Along the way, I stopped at a bakery for some crusty rolls and had a few words with the owners of a cheese store. A couple of blocks later, I chatted with a milkman delivering his product from house to house. Later, I stopped at St. Paul's Cathedral for a rest.

St. Paul's is the masterpiece of architect Sir Christopher Wren. It is considered the spiritual centre for Christians in Britain. Construction took fifty years and it is famous for the revolutionary single-domed structure, one of England's most beautiful landmarks.

At the Cathedral, I sat on the steps alongside other tourists and ate my lunch before entering the magnificent structure.

Inside, I felt spiritually lifted as I walked through this monument to the glory of God and viewed the architectural splendor and the tombs of Admiral Horatio Nelson and the Duke of Wellington.

Later, I strolled through Fleet Street and along the Thames where boats of all sizes crammed the river.

On Sunday, I walked to Buckingham Palace, Footguards' Square and Hyde Park to listen to all of the characters who stood on their step-stools on Sunday 'to have a go' at everything and everyone.

I also visited the National Maritime Museum at Greenwich and flea markets along Petticoat Lane, in Penny Lane and Abbey Road, made famous by the Beatles.

The first day of the Conference for me was taken up with getting acquainted with the other representatives on various Committees and listening to the presentations of other members.

All of the Canadian delegates were given special tickets to attend the Queen's Birthday Parade in London. Our seats along the parade route were spectacular; the Horseguards Cavalry in full dress uniform were mounted on sleek black horses.

The military bands marched by playing all of the marching music made famous during World War II. It brought back memories of the days I spent as a juvenile living in Ottawa, the capital of Canada. I recalled the many occasions during the war and on VE day when I visited the Parliament Buildings and the Cenotaph where our military bands played all of the same march music.

Prince Charles and Prince Phillip, resplendent in their uniforms, rode by on their horses some twenty feet from us. We could see the Queen and the Queen Mother in their carriages waving in their familiar manner as they passed our location. It was a sight I would never forget.

The CIA Officer and I seemed to hit it off from the start. We had a lot to talk about one evening at the cocktail party hosted by the British contingent in Grosvenor Square.

After the party, we decided to walk back to our hotels. It was dark and the large trees were bending to and fro from a brisk wind. A short distance away, we stopped in front of a Rolls Royce dealership to stare through the glass at the luxurious automobiles. The prices were around $25,000 Pounds (about $55,000 Canadian). It took my breath away; that was about five years salary.

While we were checking out the extravagant prices, we heard the sound of a car horn, actually a soft beep. Behind us, in a small yellow and black two door car, sat two very attractive women I guessed were in their late twenties.

"Hello chaps, can we give you a lift?" said the woman behind the wheel.

My CIA friend and I stared at each other and he said, "We're on our way back to our hotels a few blocks away."

"Come on, get in. We'll take you there," said her friend.

We looked at each other and nodded. I got into the back seat with one of the women and my CIA pal sat in the passenger's seat up front.

Their skirts barely covered their thighs. The woman in the driver's seat started up the car, drove ahead about ten yards and stopped.

"Were you chaps going anywhere tonight?"

I replied, "One of the guys at our cocktail party gave us the name of a private club he thought we would enjoy."

"You don't have to go to a club for a good time," said the woman sitting beside me. She handed me a business card for an escort service.

She explained that they were just patrolling around looking for some customers. "We don't charge very much and we have some special services."

"How much?" I said.

"$100 pounds for two hours, sixty pounds for one hour."

I had expected that answer. They were attractive, young hookers. My CIA pal gave me a knowing look. We decided to go along with this, to see how far it could go. We had about eighty pounds cash between us. I wasn't interested but I was curious.

"What hotel are you staying at?"

My CIA pal gave them the name of his hotel.

"We can't go there. They know us."

"I'm at the Trafalgar," I said.

"That would be better."

"We only have about thirty pounds", I lied. "That's all." In the back of my mind, I thought about the reaction it would have if they really came to my hotel and we were seen by the other Canadian delegates.

"Too bad," said the blonde in the driver's seat. "It's not negotiable!" She reached over and opened the door. We got out and stood by the open window.

"I thought you were going to drop us off at our hotel."

"Ta, ta, Chaps," she said as they drove away.

We looked at each other, then stared at the hotel about two blocks away and bent over laughing.

The next evening at one of the receptions, my 'so-called CIA friend' had everyone in stitches as he graphically outlined the events of the previous night.

One of the wives of a British Naval Commander looked at me with a twinkle in her eye and said "Isn't a British woman worth sixty pounds?" I was at a loss for words and wisely kept my mouth shut!

On the third day of the Conference, my paper was discussed at length particularly by the Ministry of Defence (MODUK) delegates and there were some lively exchanges. I was also very interested in a discussion about the Russian introduction of Ropucha-class Roll-on/Roll-off (Ro-Ro) cargo ships presented by a U.S. Navy representative. It was the first time I had heard of these vessels and their potential use by the Soviet Navy.

Built in Poland in the early 1970s, these new construction-prepositioning ships were used to carry large numbers of troops, vehicles and supplies and enhanced Russia's long range amphibious capability.

I attended all of the CANUKUS Conferences in Washington, Ottawa and London between 1977 and 1984.

In 1977, I also made my first visit to Maritime Command (MARCOM) Headquarters in Halifax to discuss Foreign Maritime Operations off Canada. One of the subjects we discussed involved the possibility of Foreign Fishing Trawlers and Research Vessels dropping off agents in Halifax or St. Johns.[19]

My first visit to our intercept site at Canadian Forces Station in Gander, Newfoundland in 1978 gave me an opportunity to discuss their monitoring of foreign vessels operating in Canadian territorial waters. During the visit I experienced the Newfoundland tradition of being 'Screeched-In'.

In 1979, I made the usual side visit for pre-conference SIGINT discussions with my counterparts at GCHQ in Cheltenham, England. After those sessions, I hopped a train to London and checked into the Regent Palace Hotel in Piccadilly Square. With a weekend free to explore more of the countryside outside of the Capital, I decided to take a bus out to Hampton Court Palace. I had heard that it was a marvelous structure in a beautiful setting in the English countryside.

---

19   Discussions with MARCOM staff led to the plot for my first novel 'A Spy
       Too Close' written in the late 1980s and published in 2005

The Palace is located in the London Borough of Richmond upon Thames, in Middlesex County. In the early 1500s it was the home of Henry VIII. Its spacious gardens and collections of furniture, arms and art, including murals, paintings and tapestries makes it a top tourist attraction.

In 1986, a major fire destroyed much of the King's Apartment Section. Restorations took four years to complete.

When I stepped off the bus, I was astounded by the size and grandeur of the Palace. I headed for the ticket office and stopped in my tracks. There standing in front of me was Jaclyn Smith, one of the U.S. Television stars of 'Charley's Angels'. I recognized the tall man with blond hair standing beside her, but couldn't put a name to the face. I later found out that he was her then current husband, Dennis Cole, another well-known actor in the same era.

She was as perfect and yet more beautiful than she appeared on the television screen!

I grabbed my camera and was about to take a photograph when the man accompanying them rushed over and said in a very thick English accent, "Please, sir don't make a fuss. They're on a delayed honeymoon and would like some privacy."

I cursed inwardly and said, "Okay." I put the camera back in its case.

After buying a ticket I visited the castle, hanging back behind her group as we meandered through the high-ceiling halls and the unbelievable tapestries. I could pick up a few comments from the guide as he stopped to point out the historical significance of each of the treasures.

At the end of the tour, I followed the three of them as we all exited into the spacious gardens. They turned left as I swung right to head for the bus stop.

Ms. Smith turned around and shouted, "Thank you so much!"

When I got off the bus a few blocks from the British Museum, I decided to tour this historic London landmark which was displaying the Guttenburg Bible.

While reading one of the pages, I heard an Englishman describing the bible in a rather high pitched tone. I turned my head to see if he would lower his voice.

There, standing a couple of feet to my left was Jackie Kennedy—actually Onassis, since her last marriage. I was spellbound to say the least.

She asked questions in such a soft voice, so low that I could barely hear the words. We were there for about ten minutes before her entourage turned to leave. I moved back to the wall, trying not to draw attention to myself as I made my way to the front entrance to get a photograph.

After a few minutes, I finally realized that they had taken her through another private exit to avoid the crowds. How disappointing.

However, I kept thinking 'What a stroke of luck. Two famous women on the same day and they were both named Jackie!" But, I was very disappointed that I couldn't get either of their photographs.

One of the highlights arranged by Ministry of Defence staff was a tour of Winston Churchill's Bunker and War Room below London. The bunker was created to provide a safe place for Churchill and his Cabinet to retreat if the UK Government offices and Ministries at Whitehall were bombed by the Germans.

It was a gloomy dark place with tunnels running every which way. We saw the Conference, Communications and Operations Rooms. The latter contained maps of various theatres of war.

It was interesting to see the tunnels in which machine gun positions were set up in case German troops entered London and found the underground passages leading to the Bunker.

At the Conference, I presented an update on the Soviet nuclear- powered Arktika icebreaker which emphasized the impact these vessels could have on development of the Arctic both economically and militarily.

TWELVE

During the next year, I was preparing two papers (classified) for the CANUKUS Maritime Conference in Washington in May 1980.

Rumours were circulating around CSE; a position I had also aspired to fill was becoming available. I asked my Senior Manager to consider me for the soon-to-be vacant position.

In April 1980, I was called into his office and informed that the job was mine. It meant a promotion to Communications Officer 4 Level but equally important to me was the fact that I *really* wanted the job. Before I would take over, however, I was informed that the Chief of CSE wanted to speak to me.

I was a bit curious about the meeting. The Chief had been my boss in Washington nine years earlier. I couldn't figure out what the meeting had to do with my promotion.

I was in for a surprise.

My Senior Manager escorted me to the Chief's office. The Chief told me he was pleased that I had accepted the promotion and then he threw me a bombshell.

"You have been selected to head up a special Signals Intelligence team which will participate in the 1980 NATO Atlantic Exercise Teamwork-80 in September."

I was mesmerized. I felt like jumping up and shouting "Yes!"

Radio operators would be seconded from the Canadian Forces Supplementary Radio System (CFSRS) at the Canadian Forces Station (CFS) Leitrim. We would spend three weeks at sea on a Canadian Destroyer providing real-time support to the Canadian Admiral who would be heading up the Orange Force (enemy) against the Blue Force (friendly, i.e. U.S.).

There would be more than 100 ships and many aircraft participating. The Soviets were expected to monitor the exercise from their destroyers, frigates and TU-95 turboprop-powered strategic bombers (NATO designation BEAR) and Tupolev TU-22M fighters.

Never having been to sea, I welcomed the opportunity. My answer: "I would be pleased to accept that task and the appointment".

I felt that it was a great move to fuse SIGINT real-time support to an ongoing operation. All participating organizations would benefit from the results.

I spent the next two months preparing for the CANUKUS Maritime Conference in Washington, D.C. in June and the NATO exercise in September. In July1980, I would assume my new position as head of a team of analyst/reporters in a highly-classified area. Our mandate was to provide intelligence on foreign naval deployments and operations in the Arctic Ocean and on vessels deployed off the coasts of Canada and the U.S.

During my tenure in CSE, I was cognizant of the interaction between various Soviet entities operating in the Arctic. Soviet scientists and naval-related researchers were believed to be involved in under-ice research including measurements of the bottom topography and ocean depths.

Since I also attended many of the related discussions at previous CANUKUS Maritime Conferences, I was familiar with foreign world-wide naval operations. So, I set my goals to complete my current responsibilities and prepare for a new challenge. Fortunately, I had already been involved in discussions with many of the British, American and Canadian military organizations and personnel with whom I had maintained close contact.

In May 1980, I attended the SIGINT meetings at NSA and was humbled by the US and UK representatives who welcomed me into their fold. Prior to the Maritime Conference scheduled for the following week, I was invited to visit the U.S. Naval Ocean Surveillance Center (NOSIC) in the Navy Field Operational Intelligence Office (NFOIO) in Suitland, Maryland. A Conference delegate with whom I had discussed the Warsaw Pact use of Roll-On/Roll-Off vessels at a previous meeting also gave me a briefing. He was scheduled to present a paper at the 1981 Maritime Intelligence Conference in Ottawa.[20]

As the time for my departure for the NATO exercise approached, I had to come up with a cover story to explain my long absence from my family. I told them that I would be involved in a special exercise in the U.K. for about three weeks. By 1980, they were accustomed to the fact that I

---

20   CIA-246 declassified document, Naval History and Heritage Command, U.S. Navy, June 1981

was attending conferences in London and Washington on a regular basis. If any serious family matters arose, they had the names and telephone numbers of CSE personnel who could get in touch with me.

THIRTEEN

A couple of days after the Orange/Blue Exercise, we sailed past the Azores. The *Athabaskan* took a turn at leading the entire convoy. I wasn't sure if it had any special significance. Was it a normal practice or were we rewarded with taking the lead of the convoy on the basis of our success during the Orange/Blue exercise? I had forgotten to ask.

When I was on the aft deck of the Athabaskan with our team and some of the crew, I watched the *Nimitz* following us at close quarters. It was like a ten storey apartment building bobbing up and down behind a canoe!

I turned to the First Officer and said, "Would you please ask the Captain to keep his foot down on the gas pedal. If that thing catches us we'll look like a bunch of match sticks."

North of the Azores, we were joined by vessels of the other NATO countries (British, Dutch, German and Norwegian Forces) involved in TW-80. As we moved north in convoy formation, the *Athabaskan* and *Ottawa* were involved in a demonstration of a unique Canadian method of refueling-at-sea by the Canadian tanker HMCS *Protecteur*.

A number of Naval Officers from other NATO countries were on board our ships to observe the operation. There was more brass on board than the entire UCLA Marching Band during the Rose Bowl Parade.

The *Athabaskan* and the *Ottawa* set similar courses about 200 yards apart. The *Protecteur* sailed through the gap and maintained pace with the two Canadian ships.

The waves were quite high but the three vessels maintained their speed and mutual pace. Then, the tanker fired lines and fuel hoses across to the two refueling vessels.

I was amazed to see the way the lines were passed across to the ships; the vessels operated at close quarters while the waves sent them high and low, to port and to starboard.

On another occasion, I watched the Sea King helicopter crews who demonstrated a 'Bear-trap' locking device on the deck of the destroyer. The Canadian invention, a haul-down system, was used for landing and securing helicopters on destroyers on a small deck in rough seas.

The Sea King hovered over the ship about fifty feet above the deck. A line was lowered from the helicopter to a crew on the deck. A heavier haul-down cable was attached and drawn up to a probe in the chopper. The haul-down cable was locked in position inside the probe, the slack was taken up and a Landing Control Officer controlled the haul-down and landing.

It was thrilling to have witnessed these operations and I was proud of the expertise and efficiency of our Navy. The visitors had smiles on their faces and some lively conversations followed.

On our way towards the west coast of England, our operators were scouring the airwaves for any radio communications between two Soviet aircraft operating in the area.

We were all excited. This is exactly why we were here, the reason for our involvement, and it was actually happening. We gathered around the operator while he listened on his headset. He finally picked up the conversation.

The CFSRS leader and I both put on a headset and listened to the two pilots' exchanges.

"Get the Captain and the First Officer down here," I shouted to one of our guys.

Moments later, the Captain had the headset on and grinned, "I'm actually listening to the enemy?"

I told him, "They mentioned the side numbers of both the *Nimitz* (shestdesyat vocem- #68) and the *Athabaskan* (dvesti vocem desyat dva-#282)."

The Captain's grin and comments said it all. We had shown that SIGINT could furnish timely support during ongoing operations at sea.

I subsequently learned that two Soviet Tupolev TU-22M fighters had overflown the exercise area and were escorted away by U.S. TOMCAT fighter aircraft.[21]

---

21   U.S. Dept. of the Navy. Naval Historical Center, Naval History and Heritage Command; Wikipedia F14 TOMCAT, Operational History, September 1980

A few days later we were told that the U.S. Admiral from the Atlantic Fleet Headquarters in Norfolk who was on board the *Nimitz* would be visiting the *Athabaskan*.

Our MARCOM staff arranged for our helicopter to pick up the Admiral. When the Admiral's helicopter landed on the Athabaskan, his first comment was, "I would like to speak to those intelligence guys you have on board."

I don't know how he knew we were aboard. Perhaps it was part of the exercise and our Captain had told him.

The Captain escorted him below deck to our cramped quarters.

The Admiral said, "I just wanted to meet all of you and commend you for your excellent work during the Orange/Blue operation. I have already advised Norfolk HQs of your success and our shortcomings. I've asked them to look at the methods you used. I'm personally sending letters of commendation to your respective agencies."

He went to each man on our team and shook his hand. When he was introduced to me, he noticed that I was wearing civilian clothing, grinned and said, "Congratulations on a job well done."

I guess he was surprised to see a civilian in the group. I was speechless. Well, almost. "Thank you, sir" I replied, beaming from ear to ear.

As the Admiral was leaving, the Captain of the Athabaskan leaned over and whispered, "Would you like to accompany the Admiral back to the *Nimitz*."

"Yes, Sir!"

I followed the entourage up to the main deck and headed for the chopper. I was hopeful of getting a chance to fly on a chopper before the end of the NATO exercise. But, this was more than I expected.

I climbed into the helicopter and sat beside the Admiral's Aide. Our conversations were limited by the sounds of the props but the Admiral was curious about where I worked.

"The Communications Security Establishment; we're the NSA counterpart in Canada."

He smiled, and said. "I suspected that there was a connection."

As we approached the *Nimitz*, I was awed by its enormity. The Aide told me there were more than 7,000 men on board the multi-decked ship. I could not believe the number of aircraft scattered around the main deck.

After we landed, I stepped onto the deck. I was stunned when I saw the rows of F-14 TOMCAT fighters and helicopters strung along the deck measuring about three football fields (American) long. The Admiral shook my hand and nodded to me as I got aboard the helicopter. One of the *Nimitz'* crew handed me a cap as a souvenir of my trip (see image 22).

On our way back, the aircrew told me that there was a Soviet Krivak-class Naval Frigate following the convoy.

A few minutes later, the pilot shouted, "Over there, on the right!"

I turned and looked down just as we were passing over its stern. I noticed that some of the crew on the Soviet vessel were taking photos of us.

The appearance of the Russian Frigate was not unexpected. Soviet and Warsaw Pact vessels used the NATO Exercises to monitor the West's operational techniques and also to train their Navy personnel.

The next day, the NATO convoy moved past the UK where we witnessed a near disaster. While our team was on the upper deck taking a group photograph (the only photo we took), we observed a ship-to-ship transfer of a package between the *Athabaskan* and a U.S. vessel.

Suddenly, the package fell into the water and we were passing it.

The ship lurched and started to turn sharply to port. We held on tight then scrambled down to the main deck. One of the crew said that the package contained the report on the activities of the Canadian ships in the first phase of the NATO exercise.

The *Krivak* was closing on us and could easily retrieve the package. The *Athabaskan* was turning to block the *Krivak*.

In a short time, a motorized Zodiac raft with two Athabaskan sailors aboard was lowered into the water and racing towards the package. They reached it before the Soviet vessel did!

It could have been an embarrassment for the Canadian Navy, but the prompt action by the crew averted a disaster.

The next day, when we were approaching the Shetland Islands, the Russian Frigate was following us at close range. The Commander directed his photographer to take us up with him in the helicopter 'for a look-see'.

The CFSRS leader and I jumped onto the chopper and they strapped us into harnesses. As we passed over the Soviet vessel, I stared down at their crew members who were also taking photos of us.

My only thought was, "I wonder what they'll think when they develop those photos and notice that one of the passengers is wearing a pair of brown checkered pants. Hmmm. Maybe they'll think I was from the CIA?"

What a thrilling experience!

Just watching the entire Canadian formation led by the *Athabaskan* and the majestic *Nimitz* crashing through the waves behind us became an indelible memory for me.

To my knowledge, it was the first time that CSE was involved in an ongoing SIGINT support mission at sea during a NATO Exercise. Some of the MARCOM support staff on board and the *Athabaskan* crew took photos, but our team was not included.

The next few days were routine as the ships entered the Norwegian Sea and the exercise ended.

The *Athabaskan* headed to Newcastle Upon Tyne, England. Sailing down the Tyne River towards the port of Newcastle, I was shocked at the conditions I saw along the route. Apparently, the shipbuilding industry in the area was suffering and unemployment was at its highest level.

The people lined the banks, waved at the ship and shouted greetings to us.

As we approached the port, the Captain informed us that he would be hosting the Mayor and other dignitaries from the City of Newcastle. Our team was certainly looking forward to the event.

I was scheduled to disembark at Newcastle that night and head to London the next day. After packing, I put on a suit and joined the CFSRS group who were, of course, still in uniform'.

I got quite a ribbing about the suit.

We were introduced to the Mayor, his entourage and Newcastle City officials.The hors d'oeuvres were great. Although the food on the ship had been pretty good during the three weeks on board, this food was a welcome change.

I noticed that one of the CFSRS guys was coming in my direction, escorting an attractive young woman.

"I told this young lady that we had a 'James Bond-type' on board and she asked for an introduction."

As I shook her hand, I could feel my face blushing red. I figured that she was no more than twenty-two, about the same age as my eldest daughter.

"Tell me all about yourself," she said.

"Well, I like my beer stirred, not shaken."

She laughed aloud, "Now that's original."

I gave her a general rundown, the unclassified version with a few embellishments. We had a drink in the corner and talked about Canada and Newcastle. She was a steno in the Mayor's office.

I noticed that some of the crew members were giving us the 'fish-eye look' - not too pleased that I was dominating her time.

I also met a few of the town's officials, but I was anxious to get ashore. After my time on board the ship, I was looking forward to a nice warm comfortable bed at my hotel that night.

While I was asking the First Officer to call me a cab, I heard a soft female voice behind me. "It's not that far. I'm heading that way. We can walk there."

It was the young secretary.

"Sure. That would be nice."

The First Officer had an odd grin on his face when he saw my young escort walking behind me, carrying my small briefcase. I could almost read his mind.

"Nice to have had you aboard, Mr. Lawruk. Thank you and your team for making our mission successful. Have a good trip home."

I walked down to the street level dragging my suitcase and chatting to the young woman, heading for the hotel. Above me, on the main deck, stood all of the CFSRS guys holding beers, whistling and shouting, "We'll be over to see you at the hotel."

They did. But I was in bed. I never had the opportunity to tell them that when we arrived at the hotel I put her in a taxi and sent her home. I let them use their own imagination.

I arrived in London the next morning and settled into my hotel near Piccadilly Circus in the heart of the city. Greenwich was on my sight-seeing schedule followed by my favourite activity – walking around London. That night, I visited the Nell Gwynne Pub and sat at the bar.

A couple of young lads sitting beside me noticed my Canadian flag lapel pin. One of them said "You from Canader, mate?"

"Yes."

The second fellow said, "I'm Mike and this is Stan. Got a sister in Toronto. You from there? Maybe you know her? Name's Louise Miller."

"No, I live in Ottawa. It's about 500 kilometers from Toronto."

I loved their Cockney accents but I had a hell of a time understanding what they said.

They were surprised when I told them that I was a big fan of the Tottenham Hotspurs soccer team which was based in London. I seemed to have hit a nerve.

We talked for a long time and they learned that I was alone. Before I left, they asked me if I wanted to come to a barbeque the next evening in Kent, an hour south of London by train.

It sounded like fun, so I agreed. They gave me the directions and the number of the train I should take. "Dress casually, it's a Sixties party! We'll meet you at the station around 5 p.m."

The next day, after exploring more of London, I picked up a box of chocolates. The English love their sweets. I put on a pair of Jeans, rolled up the sleeves of my white T-shirt and greased up my hair.

When I arrived at the station in Kent both of the guys and their girlfriends were there to meet me. The men were wearing tight white T-shirts and Stan had an Elvis hairdo.

The two women were dressed (literally) in miniskirts showing off their great legs and loose, low-cut blouses. They were very attractive. I guessed that they were in their late twenties or early thirties.

When we arrived at the party, the backyard was decorated and lit by torches. My nostrils picked up the scent of steaks on the barbeque. I was surprised to see that their way of life wasn't much different than ours.

It was a splendid night and they were great hosts. At 12:30 a.m., I told them that I would have to leave. I had a flight the next morning and would have to catch the next train back to London.

I could sense that there was something wrong.

"There are no trains to London after midnight."

Gulp. I was in trouble. "How can I get back?"

"Why don't you stay here overnight and take the morning train back."

I certainly didn't want to miss my flight home. "Any other time and I would jump at the chance."

"Okay, we'll call you a cab."

I gave them my address and asked them to get in touch with me if they ever came to Ottawa.

After thanking them for a wonderful evening I got into the taxi and headed for London. It took forty-five minutes to get to my hotel and cost me twenty-five British pounds, about $40.00 Canadian. But it was worth it!

The next day I caught the Canadian Forces flight back to Canada.

Ten days after I returned to CSE, I was given a copy of the letter sent by the Commander-in-Chief of the Atlantic Fleet at Norfolk, Virginia, congratulating me and my team for our accomplishments against the *Nimitz* during TW-80. The letter was given to the CSE Personnel Office to be placed on my personal file. I never saw it again. I would like to have had it as a reminder of one of the most exciting events in my life.[22]

It wasn't the last time I would see the *Nimitz*. In 1998, while returning to Canada from our winter home in Arizona, my wife Merla and I took a side trip to visit the Nimitz Museum in Fredericksburg, Texas. Besides the memorabilia involving the aircraft carrier, the museum included: a large mock-up of the *Nimitz* enclosed in a glass cage, a Japanese Zero aircraft hanging overhead and a copy of the papers that Admiral Nimitz signed when Japan surrendered in 1945.

In 2006, we visited the San Diego Marine Museum and toured the aircraft carrier *USS Midway*. From the deck of the *Midway* we could see the *Nimitz* (see image 23) anchored in the Bay.

We also walked through a Russian FOXTROT-class attack submarine (see image 24) used as a museum. In its time, the attack submarine was considered to be one of the finest non-nuclear submarines to have been built.

We were shocked to see the limited space for the crew; some bunks were right beside the Torpedoes (see image 25) and the Torpedo Launch Tubes (see image 26). I also checked out the periscope (see image 27).

---

22   Only three years after TEAMWORK-80, A Petty Officer on the Nimitz in the 1980s became involved in one of the most damaging spy rings in U.S. history; see Chapter Seventeen.

22. Author wearing Nimitz Cap

23. USS NIMITZ, San Diego Bay

24. Russian FOXTROT submarine in San Diego Harbour

25. Torpedoes on FOXTROT Submarine

26. Launch Tubes on FOXTROT Submarine

27. Periscope on the FOXTROT Submarine

FOURTEEN

In 1981, the CANUKUS Maritime Intelligence Conference shifted to Ottawa. I was a CSE delegate and also a Coordinator for the SIGINT sessions at the Tilley Building preceding the Conference. That fall, my former supervisor and I successfully grieved our positions as CO3 Supervisors and were promoted to the CO4 level. Our success was another trail-blazer for other CSE Communication Officers at that level who were later promoted to CO4s.

At about this time I was experiencing some restless moments in my life. When my children were young, I decided that despite my doubts about the strength of my marriage, I couldn't leave them without a father. My travels between 1976 and 1981 had instilled an adventurous nature in me and an exposure to a different world, another way of life. However, I vowed that I would never leave my marriage until my daughters were able to stand on their own two feet.

I visited a U.S. Naval friend in San Diego, California on two occasions, in 1981 and 1982. He escorted me to a number of U.S. naval sites to get a close look at vessels and talk to some of the crews.

The UK – Falklands War forced the cancellation of the 1982 Maritime Intelligence Conference. Nonetheless, my Senior Manager decided that I should visit GCHQ for discussions. He also arranged for my visit to the British Signals Intelligence station at Scarborough on the northeast coast, to see how they handled their coverage of foreign vessels operating in and around the British Isles. It was felt that we could learn much from our British partners on these operations.

After a successful three day session with our counterparts at GCHQ, I took the train northeast past Bristol and York to the countryside of Yorkshire and the City of Scarborough.

The next morning, while jogging along the coast road I was impressed with the location, the fishing village and the Roman ruins high on the cliffs where the spas were located. It was a truly unique site.

The sessions with the British operators were most enlightening. I was able to compare their target coverage with ours and the methods they used to intercept Foreign naval targets, particularly the Sovet naval vessels that moved between the Barents Sea and the North Atlantic.

In the case of Soviet submarines and Naval SIGINT collection vessels, we were interested in their presence in or near Canadian territorial waters. The Soviets first used Fishing Fleet vessels for intelligence collection purposes then introduced naval vessels with sophisticated SIGINT and Electronic Intelligence equipment. In addition to the Soviet Navy's hydrographic research program, they provided sophisticated electronic support to their surface and submarine fleets.

While conducting reconnaissance missions against NATO exercises and ports, and U.S./Canadian joint exercises, these spy ships were believed to be capable of identifying the signatures and noise patterns of Western submarines and surface vessels.

In the mid-1980s we began using desktop terminals and developing our computer skills. It was a far cry from our previously written or typed drafts of our reports and technical papers. Eventually, everything was input to the data bases by analysts and reporters.

In 1983, I decided that it was time to leave my marriage. It was one of the worst periods in my life; the effect it had on my daughters almost broke my heart. Despite the shock to all of us, I remained close to both of my girls and we eventually regained our close relationships and love for one another.

The 1983 Signals Intelligence Sessions at GCHQ in Cheltenham and the CANUKUS Maritime Intelligence Conference in London were held in May-June. I was joined by the CSE Officer who had assumed my former job. At one of the sessions, I discussed the requirements for CSE reporting on various foreign operations (classified) and the inclusion of 'Analyst Comments' in our product.

At the pre-CANUKUS SIGINT sessions, I created a bit of a stir when I informed them that a close friend of mine in Canada gave me $100 to bet on a horse running at the Cheltenham racecourse that week. When the horse won, everyone was sorry they didn't put a few 'bob' on it as well.

I had an opportunity to observe a steeplechase race on a later occasion and had purchased a ticket. The odds on the horse were 18 to 1.

I was surprised to see that the races ran in a clockwise direction, as opposed to the North American counter-clockwise method. My horse had the lead as the field completed the first half of the race. I was pretty excited but my friends suggested that I wait a while before celebrating.

Suddenly, the horses all disappeared from sight. I was shocked. One of the people beside me said the track dropped into a small valley before turning for the final home stretch.

Then, out of the mist appeared my horse, still in front, but faltering. He had trouble on the hill leading up to the home stretch - and finished fifth! Such was my introduction to English-style horse racing.

One evening we also joined a group of GCHQ staff on a 'Donnington Run' named after a village in Gloucestershire, famous for its 'Donnington Ale'. The tour involved a visit to many of the 15 pubs in the area. I can't remember how many we visited, but when I woke up the next morning I knew I had made a lot of them. According to the locals, I was surprised to learn that, up to that time at least, the fabulous ale was not exported outside the 'shire'.

Four days later, I checked into the Charing Cross Hotel in London and went out with a couple of the guys for dinner. They returned to their hotel and because I love to dance, I decided to go to a Disco Club.

I met a group of Finnish stewardesses; they were friendly, lovely, blond and tall. We sat in one corner of the crowded dance club and talked about Canada and Finland. I had noticed this attractive redhead standing near the bar and decided to ask her for a dance.

We seemed to hit it off even though she spoke in broken English. She said that she was from East Germany and was working as an Assistant to the Attache at their Embassy. I told her I worked for the Canadian Government.

She was planning a car trip to Brighton the following day and asked me if I wanted to join her. Having nothing planned until Monday when the Conference began, I agreed.

She picked me up at my hotel at the Charing Cross Rail Station early Saturday morning in her MG and we headed for the coast. It was an interesting trip through the English countryside and we talked about a lot of different things, but nothing about work.

After walking along the Brighton seashore, we picked up some fish and chips wrapped in newspaper. When we passed the Grand Hotel, I realized that only five years earlier Prime Minister Margaret Thatcher had narrowly escaped an assassination attempt at that site. We drove back to London later in the evening and she dropped me off at my hotel.

We spent Sunday at Hyde Park listening to the goofy, but colourful characters preaching from their little wooden boxes. They covered subjects as diverse as British politics, gays (they refer to them as 'puffs'), immigrants in England, the Church, and even insulted each other. Nothing was sacred!

On Monday night, after the first day of the Conference, I joined five members of our Canadian contingent for dinner at a local pub. We returned to the hotel around 8:30 and went directly to our rooms.

When I got to my room on the second floor, I discovered that my door was open. I was even more shocked when I realized that the frame around the door had actually been pried off.

I went into the room and headed for the closet. I always hid my camera under a shirt or sweater hanging in the closet. It had worked before and this time was no exception. I never left anything valuable in my room at least not in the open or in the drawers-and certainly not any money.

I notified the front desk and called the Senior DDI staff member who was also staying on the same floor. He beat the Manager to my room and we went over it again. I had already checked the phone and the lights for any bugs or any unusual wires. They moved me to a room on the third floor.

I wondered how anyone could make that much damage without someone else hearing the noises. No one had called the front desk. Was it one man? An attempted robbery? The extent of the damage indicated that someone would have had to act as a lookout in case other guests walked by the room.

Another intriguing thought was that the red-haired German woman was the only person outside of the CANUKUS community that knew I was with the Canadian Government and at which hotel I was staying. When I tried to contact her, no one answered the phone and there was no recorded message. I never heard from her again.

It was a long shot, but I tended to lean towards a thief with lots of guts!

The incident created a lighter note. At one of the Conference cocktail parties, a British delegate's wife had a grin on her face when she commented, "I heard that the British women are breaking down the doors to get to you. What's your secret?"

Returning to Ottawa on the Canadian Forces flight from London the following Monday, I was left with one thought. What were they looking for?

I still feel uneasy about the incident because there were four other fellow delegates on the same floor and their rooms were not breached. It remains a mystery.

One of the more chilling moments experienced by a few of the CSE staff in the Tilley Building occurred in 1983. On September 1st, a staff member ran into the hall to tell other staff members that he had just heard about the shooting down of a civilian passenger airliner.

The whole floor was buzzing. That turned out to be a South Korean KAL Flight 007 which was shot down by a Russian SU-15 interceptor. KAL 007 excerpts were eventually released and subsequently mentioned in the NSA document '60 Years Defending Our Nation'.

In 1983, I was elected President of Manderley Golf Club located just south of Ottawa. One of the most rewarding experiences was coordinating the Muscular Dystrophy Charity Tournament which contributed about $3,000 over two years. Members and guests joined with sports personalities from the Ottawa Rough Riders and the Ottawa 67s, coached by my childhood friend Brian Kilrea.

My most exciting sports experience came in 1983 when I won the B Class (handicaps 10-14) Club Championship at Manderley and qualified to participate in the Ottawa Valley (OVGA) 'Champion of Champions' tournament at Mont St Marie Golf Club. "B" Class Champions from all of the clubs on each side of the Ontario/Quebec border were represented. I shot a 79 and won the tournament (see image 28). I received a trophy as well as a jacket from Noel Kerr Men's Store.

In 1994, two years after I joined the Mississippi Golf Club in Appleton, Ontario, west of Ottawa, I repeated the feat. I shot a 79 at the final event held at the Carleton Golf and Yacht Golf Club near Vars, south of Ottawa.

28. Winning 'B Class' Ottawa Valley Golf Championship in 1983

FIFTEEN

In May 1984, my principal responsibilities involved Foreign Naval-related Operations in the Arctic and in Canadian Coastal Regions. I was also a CSE delegate to the SIGINT discussions at NSA and the CANUKUS Maritime Conference in Washington, D.C. The Conference, hosted by the Defense Intelligence Agency (DIA) was held at Bolling Air Force Base. I had an opportunity to have in-depth discussions with my U.S. counterparts. One of the sessions pertained to the presence of Soviet SIGINT Trawlers and submarines off the east coast of Canada and the U.S.

During the years 1958 to 1984, I had covered most of the topics related to Soviet operations in the Arctic along the maritime areas of the Northern Sea Route (NSR) and the land and islands around Russia's northern border.

Using primarily open source/collateral information, I had developed a comprehensive knowledge of Soviet activities in the Arctic including:

- the provision of navigation safety in Arctic ice/waters and the Northern Sea Route (NSR);

- the improvement and seasonal extension of resupply operations to Russian communities along the NSR;

- support to military operations;

- development of data bases on hydro-meteorology, hydrology, hydro-acoustics, drifting ice research;

- airborne and marine traffic control especially for military purposes;

- aids to navigations systems in the high Arctic; and

- mapping of the Arctic Ocean floor and seamounts

I had also gained much knowledge on the Soviet Naval, Scientific, Merchant and Fishing Fleet operations in Canadian/U.S. coastal waters.

I took special interest in Russian operations in, and claims to various sectors of the Arctic. The International Oceanographic Commission reported on 34 proposals from the Soviet Department of Navigation and Oceanography pertaining to the Belov Trough (between 88.15 degrees North and 141.06 degrees East to 89.06 degrees North and 172.00 degrees East.

The feature was discovered in 1969 by a member of the Soviet Northern Fleet Hydrographic Expedition, Vasiliy Vasil'yevich Belov (1951-2000). Belov, a Naval Hydrographer, "spent many years as an officer with the North Hydrographic Expedition of the Soviet Northern Fleet. He participated in several air expeditions and carried out oceanographic expeditions in the Arctic Ocean."[23]

The report also mentioned the results of research by Soviet scientists involved in Arctic studies over the Karasik Seamont (86.43 N 61.17 E) and the Langseth Ridge (87.00N 62.00E). Dr. Marcus Langseth is an American Geophysicist.

A third report filed by the IOC presented by the Soviet Hydrographic Office concerning the Leninskiy Komsomol Seamont in the Arctic Ocean was of particular interest. The elevations were discovered "from drift-ice observations of depth in 1965 on the Soviet Northern Fleet Hydrographic Expedition."

That reference confirmed that a Naval Research group was either on a Civil Drifting Ice Base or operating on what was suspected of being a Naval Ice Base restricted to only Soviet Naval personnel or Civilian scientists working on military–related research projects.

The lack of knowledge we had about the operations of Western submarines in the Arctic exacerbated our reporting capabilities. In later years, unclassified information was released to confirm that British and American submarines had operated under the Arctic ice cap since 1958.

---

23   Open internet searches 1960-1969: on Northern Fleet Hydrographic Airborne Expeditions in the Arctic Ocean; and on Arctic drifting ice stations by International Hydrographic Organizations

Unclassified Nauticapedia reports[24] indicated that many foreign submarines, including Soviet, American and British submarines, operated in the Canadian Sector between 1958 and 1990. Subsequent unclassified details released on the operations of the U.S. and UK subs have disclosed that some of these boats were also in close proximity to both the Kara and Barents Seas and the area around Novaya Zemlya Island.

The presence of Soviet icebreakers and Naval Hydrographic ships in the immediate area during the U.S. and/or U.K. submarine missions could have been either a reaction to these incursions or to other secret Soviet under-ice operations.

Northern Fleet Headquarters based at Severomorsk on the northern edge of the Kola Peninsula, includes DELTA III class strategic submarines (SSBNs), equipped with sea-launched ballistic missiles with nuclear warheads. Two other submarine bases are located near Murmansk at Gadzhiyevo and at Olenya.[25]

The Soviet boats use the Kola Gulf to enter the Barents Sea on their deployments to the Arctic and/or the Atlantic Ocean. From 1990, all of the Northern Fleet subs were at Gadzhiyevo.

Vladivostok, the largest Soviet port on the Pacific Ocean, located near the Chinese and Korean borders, is the home base for the Soviet Pacific Fleet Headquarters.

Unclassified sources indicate that Soviet submarines were suspected to have operated under the ice since the late 1950s. The nuclear submarine Leninsky Komsomol travelled under the Arctic ice and surfaced at the North Pole on 17 July1962. The Russians claim that their submarines have visited the Polar region on more than 300 occasions throughout the Cold War. The Arctic ice became a bastion, a sanctuary for Soviet submarines to avoid anti-submarine warfare threats from Western air and surface forces.

Four new classes of Soviet submarines operated in the Arctic: a Kilo-class in 1981, an Oscar-class cruise missle-equipped (SSGN) in 1981, a Typhoon-class ballistic missle-equipped (SSBN) in 1983 and a Yankee-class SSGN in1985.

24   A List of Underwater Transits of the Canadian Northwest Passage 1958 to 2009, Nauticapedia; North Pole Drifting Stations 1930-1980s; Arctic High Latitude Air Expeditions, 1930s-1950s; Woods Hole Oceanographic Institution

25   Wikipedia: DELTA-class Submarines, The Northern Fleet

Some of the most recent (Circa 1980) missions were inter-fleet transfers from the Northern Fleet to the Rybachiy submarine base in the Kamchatka Peninsula in the Pacific Ocean. The first such transfer was successfully made when two nuclear Northern Fleet submarines journeyed under the Arctic ice cap and reached the Pacific Fleet in September 1963.

A 6 December 2011 article published in the Canadian newspaper The Globe and Mail updated an earlier report indicating that "Soviet submarines may have routinely operated in the Canadian Sector of the Arctic during the Cold War. Charts published by the Soviet Hydrographic Service were in some cases more detailed than the Canadian versions and included knowledge of internal waterways such as the Northwest Passage."[26]

The article quoted two Canadians, an ice pilot and a Canadian academic/Arctic expert, who were on board the Russian owned Institute of Oceanography *Akademik Ioffe*. One of the experts commented "the only way the Soviet government could have acquired data for the charts is from submarines secretly patrolling the area."

The presence of a Soviet submarine would constitute a serious threat to Canadian sovereignty. Surface-launched ballistic missiles fired from the Lawrence Sea or Davis Strait would threaten our national security.

A Soviet permanent drifting ice station was believed to be associated not only with naval research in the Arctic but it may also have provided support to Soviet under-ice operations. Hydro-acousticians and hydrographers from the Northern Fleet Hydrographic Expedition were stationed on the island which floated over the troughs and ridges of the Arctic.

Soviet scientists on all of their Ice Bases were believed to have developed an Arctic bathymetry base, seafloor relief and bottom topographical charts of the valleys, ridges and hollows of the Gakkel and Lomonosov Ridges.

Ice-based programs and suspected operations by Soviet nuclear submarines and nuclear deep-water stations were conducted as early as the 1960s. These operations may have been some of the earliest missions related to the charting of the continental shelf below the ice in an effort to define the region expected to be claimed by the Soviet Union. The details provided by the Canadian Press article mentioned earlier could indicate that the Soviet research program was far wider than anyone thought possible.

---

26 The Canadian Press, from the Archives; Russian Maps Suggest Soviet Subs Cruised Canadian Arctic; 2 Dec 2013

The Soviet data base would be used for navigation and hydrographic support to its Naval Submarine and Surface Forces along their Arctic sea frontiers and beyond.

The aforementioned data could eventually be used for application of the UN Law of the Sea when the continental shelf in the Arctic is expected to be divided among the Arctic coastal States

One of the main issues which will affect Canada's claims in the Arctic will be sovereignty issues related to the jurisdiction over the Northwest Passage and the disputed Arctic areas like the Lomonosov Ridge. So – 'Who Owns the Arctic Ocean'?[27]

Russia clearly demonstrated that they would lay claim to the area which extends from the eastern and western edges of their country to the Pole. In August 2007 the Arktika-class nuclear-powered icebreaker Rossiya escorted the Soviet Polar Research Vessel *Akademik Fedorov* to the North Pole.[28] As many as 100 scientists were on board. Two deep sea mini-submarines were lowered to the floor of the ocean where a flag of the USSR was planted.

It was heralded by the Soviets as a claim to its extended continental shelf of the Arctic Ocean bottom and a symbolic move to enhance its disputed claim to nearly half of the floor on the Arctic Ocean.

Some years later, in December 2009, NATO countries were concerned about the attempts by the Soviets to obtain an agreement with the Norwegians on the use of the Svalbard archipelago to open a scientific station at Pyramiden. The archipelago is close to the access route for Russian ships and submarines to the Atlantic Ocean and a critical location for entry by foreign ships into the Barents Sea and the Arctic Ocean.

'The Russians were not just installing a scientific station but also a presence on the archipelago.'[29] In addition to the military/defensive advantages, the economic spinoffs would be significant, particularly the potential development of petroleum exploration in the area and the forthcoming United Nations Law of the Sea decision on the international

---

27   Geology.com, December 2014. A U.S. geological survey estimates that up
      to 25% of the world's remaining oil and natural gas resources might be held
      within the sea floor of the Arctic Region

28   New York Times, 3 August 2007

29   Associated Press, 12 February 2009; and Barents Observer.com, 23
      December 2009

boundary lines to the North Pole. The Soviet presence on the Svalbard Archipelago would appear to extend those boundaries in Russia's favor.

In a series of diplomatic reactions to Canadian claims to the North Pole in 2013, Russian President Vladimir Putin announced that he was stepping up their military presence in the region.[30] Within a week, three Navy vessels, including the Petr Veliky nuclear-powered missile cruiser as well as seven support vessels and four nuclear-powered icebreakers arrived in the area of Kotelny in the New Siberian Islands.[31] By September 29 all equipment, including Navy base personnel, were delivered by helicopters and support vessels.

On 29 October 2012, the *Barents Observer* reported that a Russian Top Secret submarine had operated in the area of the Mendeleyev Ridge to prove their North Pole claim. The deep-diving vessel Losharik, Russia's 'most secret nuclear-powered submarine' was supported by the Icebreakers Dikson and Kapitan Dranitsyn. The purpose of the expedition was to use the data collected when Russia present its application to the Law of the Sea Committee. There was no information on what occurred under water.

In 1984, CSE had another important challenge for me. It was the right time to leave the Production side of CSE and pursue another aspect of Intelligence, i.e. direct liaison support to Canadian consumers.

---

30   The Guardian; Russia to Boost Military Presence in Arctic as Canada plots North Pole Claim, 10 December 2013

31   Barents Observer; In Remotest Russian Arctic, a New Navy Base, 17 September 2013

SIXTEEN

After the Maritime Intelligence Conference in 1984, I was back in Ottawa for only a month when I was informed that my Manager wanted to see me.

He said, "You have been selected as the first CSE Representative to the Department of National Defence (NDHQ) in downtown Ottawa. You will be our Liaison Officer with the Chief of Intelligence and Security staff at NDHQ."

What an opportunity! I was speechless.

The view from my office on the 19th floor of the Headquarters Building was spectacular. Situated on the east side of the famous Rideau Canal across from the National Arts Centre, I could see the Parliament Buildings, the National War Memorial in Confederation Square, the regal, castle-like Chateau Laurier Hotel across from the old historic Ottawa Union Station Building, and the Gatineau Hills beyond in Quebec.

The panorama was appreciated much more by an Ottawa boy who was proud to have lived in the city for most of his life. In the winter time when the canal is frozen it becomes the world's largest skating rink. Some 20,000 to 40,000 people skate on weekends during *Winterlude* in February.

At lunch hour, I often joined many Ottawa citizens and skated along the eight kilometer (about 5 miles) slick ice surface. Along the canal, there are rest areas, refreshment booths and fires to keep warm on cold, frosty nights.

The National Arts Centre features international artists from every walk of life, concerts, plays and Broadway shows.

As I stared across the canal towards the National War Memorial, Parliament Hill and the Canadian government buildings, I recalled the many days I spent on the Hill. I loved to watch the military parades to the Cenotaph on Confederation Square and recall the memorable day when everyone celebrated Victory in Europe on the lawn in front of the Peace Tower.

The Chateau Laurier Hotel is often believed by foreign tourists to be a castle. The landmark hotel, once a renowned Canadian National Hotel, is now within the Fairmont Hotel Chain.

The Gatineau Hills, across the Ottawa River in Quebec, is about a half hour drive north of the Capital. It has great ski areas, hiking and cycling trails, and vast forested areas. In the fall the roads to the hills are jammed with thousands of visitors wishing to view the spectacular multi-coloured trees, especially the crimson red maple leaves.

Since I would have to travel to CSE occasionally, I also had my own parking spot near the building.

From the outset, the Colonel in charge of the Directorate of Defence Intelligence (DDI) and the CIS staff treated me as one of their own. I felt right at home. I liaised between the DDI and Directorate of Scientific and Technical Intelligence officers at HQs and the CSE staff on a regular basis. Eventually, I was promoted to the Communications Officer 5 level.

As I developed the job, I provided intelligence support to various offices in NDHQ. Over the next few years many of my contacts rose to become Chief of the Defence Staff. One of them later headed the Canadian Naval Forces during DESERT STORM and the war in Iraq. Another had a home along the Rideau River where I occasionally stopped for a short visit after a day of fishing.

I had to familiarize myself with the duties and functions of each of the Offices within NDHQ in order to determine their needs and CSE's ability to furnish the desired intelligence. By the end of my first year, I had new topics of interest to build a list of DND requirements. It led me down some new and interesting paths.

In 1987, Iranian press reported that the Iraqi forces under Saddam Hussein were using poison gas against their forces and the Kurdish people in Northern Iraq.

In order for me to obtain an in-depth knowledge of the Chemical Warfare world, a DND officer arranged for a visit to the Defence Research Establishment (DRE) at Shirley's Bay west of Ottawa. I was given an in depth briefing on the newest chemicals being used, their effects and the preventative measures being taken to protect our troops.

Another query involved information on the potential acquisition of nuclear icebreakers to replace the ageing Canadian vessels used for patrolling the Northwest Passage and the Arctic Ocean.

When delivering sensitive materials to Senior Officers within NDHQ (Deputy Ministers, Generals, etc) I had some difficulty trying to convince their Secretaries that their bosses were the only ones cleared to read the highly classified and sensitive material inside. When the Officers were busy, it was also difficult when their staff asked me to leave the material on their desk and they would make sure he got it.

When the material was time-sensitive I sat in the outer office and waited. Sometimes the 'Customers' asked me questions. If I wasn't able to expand or elaborate on the subject, I promised to get a reply from the originator.

One day, a Deputy Minister read the material and immediately apologized as he rushed out of his Office. Later, he told me that the information was invaluable to him and supported DND's position on deployment of Canadian peacekeeping troops at a high level Defence meeting.

After more than four years, I returned to CSE to take on another interesting project involving one of America's most damaging spies.

In November 1988, I received a Letter of Appreciation (see image 29) and a Certificate (see image 30) from the Chief of the Intelligence Services (CIS), and a Certificate (see image 31) from the Director of Defence Intelligence (DDI), NDHQ.

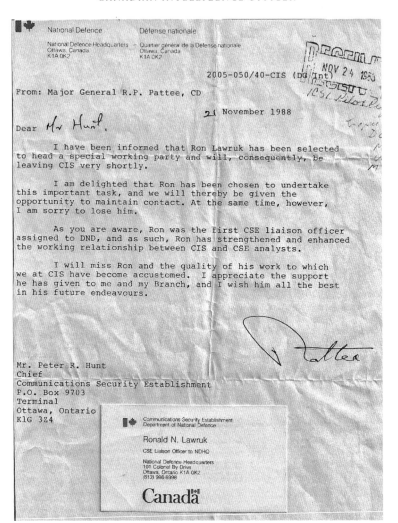

29. Letter of Appreciation from Chief of Intelligence Services, NDHQ Canada

Certificate of Appreciation

R. N. Lawruk

is awarded this certificate in recognition of service
with

Chief Intelligence and Security

during the period August 1984 *to* November 1988

Major General R.P. Pattee
CHIEF INTELLIGENCE AND SECURITY
NATIONAL DEFENCE HEADQUARTERS
OTTAWA — CANADA

30. Certificate from Chief of Intelligence Services, NDHQ Canada

31. Certificate from the Director of Defence Intelligence, NDHQ Canada.

SEVENTEEN

In 1988, after almost five years at NDHQ, I was recalled by CSE to head up a special research team responsible for assessing the impact on Canada by the John Walker Spy Ring in the U.S.

According to an article in the Naval History Magazine (June 2010, Volume 23, Number 3 by John Ramos Walker, a U.S. Naval Warrant Officer, was "the mastermind behind one of the most dangerous spy rings in U.S. history". He began his espionage career in 1967 while serving as a Watch Officer at the Atlantic Fleet Submarine Forces Headquarters in Norfolk, Virginia.

Walker was believed to have provided cryptographic secrets to the Soviets which revealed vital information on:

- tactical capabilities of the U.S. Navy nuclear submarine fleet,

- U.S. KL-47 encryption machines and

- several keylists, manuals and other highly classified and sensitive documents

The material he passed to the Russians included approximately1500 documents on weapons systems, nuclear weapons, command and control procedures, targets, etc. A Senior KGB Officer said that "the John Walker case was the greatest in KGB history".

Walker also enlisted members of his family to assist him. His son Michael, a Yeoman, stationed on the aircraft carrier Nimitz (just a couple of years after my involvement in the Teamwork 1980 Exercise) had access to vital communications information on U.S. submarine and surface vessel activities which he furnished to his father. The Soviets paid John Walker large sums of money for his unique 'contributions'.

According to the U.S. Naval History Magazine, on the 23 January 1968 the North Koreans grabbed the USS PUEBLO, an ELINT/SIGINT ship operating in their coastal waters. It is possible that Walker's information may have been passed to the North Koreans by the Russians. The acquisition of U.S. encryption equipment and codes would seem to have spurred the two Communist countries to develop their own fleet of spy ships. Both the Russian and North Korean Navies subsequently introduced vessels like the PUEBLO to their surveillance programs.

Both John Walker and his son Michael were sentenced to life in prison. The younger Walker served only fifteen years before being released. John Walker died in prison on August 28, 2014.

Two CSE officers were assigned to assist me. We had a combined total of 85 years of experience as full-time intelligence analysts and reporters.

Together with a Director of Defence Intelligence (DDI) staff from the Chief of Intelligence Services (CIS) at NDHQ, we worked closely with the U.S. Naval Intelligence offices in Washington to discuss the Walker case and its impact on Canada, the intelligence community and NATO.

A few weeks after we began the study, the Chief of CIS requested that they assume complete responsibility for the analysis and reporting on the Walker case. I was asked by the Chief of CSE, whom I considered a good friend, what I thought of the idea.

I gave him my honest opinion. "CSE analysts are more thorough and experienced than the DDI Staff who had little or no exposure to raw intelligence and most of them are not career intelligence analysts."

I quoted a statement I had often heard when I worked at the U.S. National Security Agency: "NSA provides analysis with its reports. Over time, it became evident that NSA analysts were best equipped to manage and analyze their own product."

NDHQ assumed responsibility for the project. However, I felt vindicated when my two staff members were assigned to the DDI team. I heard nothing about the eventual results of the study.

At that stage of my career, with thoughts of retirement swirling through my brain, I felt that I needed a change.

CSE Operations Centre

I was next assigned to the CSE Operations Centre (CANSOC), the SIGINT Operations Centre. Formed in 1968, CANSOC is the Canadian version of the U.S. National Security Agency's SIGINT Operations Center

(NSOC). The centralized watch centers initiate exchanges on a 24/7 basis and are essentially crisis response centres.

My job was to become familiar with worldwide events which impacted on Canada and our partners in the world-wide intelligence community. My staff and I selected significant intelligence events and any related collateral information of interest. I briefed the Chief and Senior Managers every morning.

As I mentioned earlier, during the time I visited CSE in 2011, I was impressed with the significant advances CSE had made to provide real-time support to all of its customers.

I informed CSE that I planned to retire in 1990. I assumed (or hoped) that the remaining tasks assigned to me would be those that fit my comprehensive background and experience. Therefore, I was grateful for my last full-time assignment to the "OPEN SKIES" project.

EIGHTEEN

A few months later in 1989, I was selected to represent CSE on the Canadian team during the International OPEN SKIES Conference.[32] The Chairman was none other than Joe Clark, former Prime Minister of Canada. We were briefed on the upcoming OPEN SKIES discussions between the Warsaw Pact countries and NATO. It was described as one of the most wide-ranging international efforts promoting openness and transparency of military forces and activities

Both the Pact and NATO representatives had agreed to allow official over-flights and mutual inspections of selected military bases and camps by each country involved in the OPEN SKIES program.

In the case of Canada, the first country would be Hungary.

I had many opportunities to speak with Mr. Clark and found him to be an affable, likeable person. He outlined what role CSE and the National Defence Headquarters could play in the overflights and was very precise in pointing out what he could expect from our respective intelligence organizations.

I would be responsible for submitting CSE details, outlining the methodology by which CSE could contribute real-time information and intelligence prior to and during ongoing NATO operations and for providing analysis and reporting on any operation over Warsaw Pact countries.

Our team visited Uplands Air Base in Ottawa to inspect the Challenger aircraft that Canada would be using on any inspection for which we were tasked. The aircraft would be configured to carry the required sophisticated technical and electronic equipment and the operators to man it. Our entire team was expected to fly to Hungary on the first mission.

---

32   Scheduled for 12-28 February 1990

I realized that, like my involvement in the 1980 NATO ExerciseTeamwork-80, this would be another first for CSE and an opportunity for CSE/CFSRS to supply a Canadian team during an international NATO operation.

In order for us to become familiar with the requirements of our military commands in Canada and abroad, we had to visit the various headquarters and bases. My responsibility was to bring them up to date on the role of SIGINT in support of their mission and our future role in 'OPEN SKIES'. The Officer from the Directorate of Defence Intelligence (DDI) at NDHQ and I also visited Military intelligence allies in the U.S. and the U.K.

In the U.K, we had discussions with Senior Officers at the Ministry of Defence in London, the SIGINT Staff at GCHQ in Cheltenham and specific Canadian military bases in Europe

In Germany, at the Canadian Forces Base in Lahr, and in a CF-18 bunker in Baden-Baden, the DDI officer and I briefed the pilots about the importance of intelligence collection in support of their mission.

I outlined the vast array of intelligence agencies supporting them in their defence of the Western Alliance and NATO. The primary concern of the pilots was the 'real-time actionable tactical and combat support.'

It was a unique thrill to sit and talk to the pilots. Having contracted laryngitis, I sounded like a foghorn, but I got the message across.

We also visited the Admirals and staff at Maritime Command Headquarters in Halifax, Nova Scotia and Maritime Pacific Headquarters in Esquimault, British Columbia; senior officers at Air Command HQ in Winnipeg, Manitoba and Mobile Command Headquarters at St. Hubert, Quebec.

In the latter case, after briefing the intelligence staff and the Commanding General at St. Hubert, the audience was extended to include a larger number of staff. We gave them a sanitized version of CSE and DDI's role in the world-wide intelligence community.

We also briefed them on the combined efforts of our Canadian intelligence agencies to provide timely support to our Canadian Forces abroad.

The possibility of imbedding CSE/DDI intelligence officers at forward bases was discussed at length, but at that time no specific information was available to confirm that such a program would be instituted.

In February 1990, the OPEN SKIES International Conference was held at the Canadian Congress Centre in Ottawa. OPEN SKIES involved all of the NATO and Warsaw Pact Defence Ministers as well as

U.S. Secretary of State James Baker, Messrs. Kohl and Genscher from East and West Germany respectively. Also included were hundreds of support and security personnel. Since I was on temporary assignment to National Defence Headquarters, I was listed as a member of the DDI Support Staff for the Canadian Delegation (see image 32).

All members of the Conference were invited to a cocktail party at the Russian Embassy in Ottawa. I had a dilemma. As an employee of CSE, I was forbidden to enter a Communist Country or one of their Embassies without permission. I informed the Security Officer at CSE and asked him if I could attend.

He checked it out. CSE management only agreed to allow me to attend because I was listed on the conference roster as an NDHQ employee.

As I stepped through the large steel gates of the Embassy on Charlotte Street, I had a strange feeling. As a citizen of Ottawa from birth, I had passed the building on many occasions, wondering what went on inside. On this occasion, I also thought of Igor Gouzenko, the Russian cipher clerk who defected in 1945.

Though we were restricted to the main floor foyer area, I managed to see statues of Lenin and photographs of many of the past leaders of the USSR. I couldn't help feeling nervous, wondering who was watching and what I could say.

Actually, it turned out to be pretty innocent but it remains one of the most interesting moments in my life.

During the OPEN SKIES Conference, something was obviously amiss. One day, the two German Defence Ministers were observed in animated, vigorous discussions in a corner of the hall. Everyone was waiting for them in order to start the afternoon discussions. It appeared to be very serious, but we had no idea of the possible magnitude of those discussions.

Who knows? These talks may have been related to the reunification of Germany. Within a few months, this became a reality and ultimately led to the demolition of the Berlin Wall.

There were thirty-five signatory countries to the Treaty on 'OPEN SKIES' which was "Entered into Force" on 1 January 2002. A total of 670 flights were completed between 2002 and 2010. U.S. Secretary of State

Hillary Clinton chaired the Second Treaty Review Conference in Vienna, Austria in June 2010.[33]

On 7 June 2010, Clinton said that 'the OPEN SKIES Treaty was a 'Vital Instrument for Cooperation'.

In April 1990, I decided to retire and returned to CSE. I was delighted to receive a letter of appreciation from Former Prime Minister Joe Clark (see image 33).

After thirty-two years of service to CSE, at the age of fifty-six, in June 1990 I retired. At the same time, I also received a letter from Prime Minister Brian Mulroney thanking me for my service to the Government of Canada (see image 34). It was always my plan to retire at an early age when I was still healthy. The death of my father in 1975 at the age of 63, before he could enjoy retirement, was a major factor in my decision. I wanted to travel around the world and reside in a warm climate during the winter months.

In September 1991, I was elated when a section of the Berlin Wall was placed on display in the same Government Conference Centre in which the 'OPEN SKIES' Conference was held. How appropriate, I thought. The display was subsequently moved to the Canadian War Museum in Ottawa.

In the 1990s, the Communist Bloc crumbled; perhaps the Cold War was finally over?

---

33   Open Skies Treaty, Vital Instrument For Cooperation , U.S. Secretary of State Clinton Tells Review Conference, 7 June 2010

**32. Canadian SIGINT Support Officer at 1989 NATO/
Warsaw Pact 'OPEN SKIES' Conference in Ottawa**

**33. Letter of appreciation from Former Prime Minister Joe
Clark 'OPEN SKIES' Conference in Ottawa.**

117

Ronald N. Lawruk

*On the occasion of your retirement
from the Public Service,
I wish to thank you on behalf
of the Government and people of Canada
for 32 years of loyal service
and to extend to you
our best wishes.*

June 4, 1990

Prime Minister

34. Canadian Prime Minister Mulroney Letter, 1990

EPILOGUE

During my research into the history of SIGINT and related activities by the Soviet Union, while scouring the Internet, I came across much 'open source' information. This enabled me to describe activities which, in previous years, was classified or restricted.

One example is the report titled, '60 Years of Defending Our Nation' by the U.S. National Security Agency. The report covered many of the significant factors of SIGINT: real time reporting, maintaining crypto capabilities needed to protect the nation, the concept of remoting –the collection of foreign signals from stationary facilities which required a high cost.

I believe that much of the current information available on the Internet answers some of those questions. In many cases, it seemed to fit like a glove.

To me, the most significant information involved the operations of U.S. and British submarines in the Arctic. A number of their under-ice operations in the Arctic were conducted and kept secret.

However, as a member of the CANUKUS intelligence community- but also from a Canadian sovereignty perspective-we had a responsibility to report on activities which were related to all foreign operations in the Arctic, and Soviet reactions to foreign incursions into its territorial waters.

Had some of this classified information been shared with us, perhaps we could have allocated more resources to report on Soviet reactions to foreign incursions. It would have lent more credence to our targeting and reporting programs and could have assisted both the Ministry of Defence in the UK and the Defense Department in the U.S. even more.

One can only assume that high level restrictions on these operations were ordered to maintain complete secrecy, to conceal the operation and to protect the personnel involved.

From our viewpoint, when Soviet Naval Research Vessels were accompanied by Ministry of the Merchant Fleet icebreakers, especially the nuclear-class units, there was no way to determine if the operation was simply normal hydrographic, hydro-meteorological and/or ice research activities.

Experienced members on my staff wanted to label the activities as support to Soviet Naval Research or underice operations. Lacking any evidence of a Western submarine operating in the area, we could only assume that the activities were in support of a Soviet operation.

During my thirty-two years at CSE/CBNRC, we were advised that our military customers preferred that SIGINT reports include only the facts we could prove with no analytical interpretation or conclusions. However, I eventually obtained permission to allow my reporters to add an 'Analyst Comment' to our reports if it was relevant.

In retrospect, after examining hundreds of Soviet reports and scientific publications that have recently been released covering that period, I believe it was unfortunate that we were not provided (through the appropriate channels, of course) any Western-related activities which took place within Soviet Arctic territorial boundaries. Any threat to the Western-based submarine presence by the Soviets would surely have been reported and flagged at the appropriate level.

This was particularly relevant to U.K. and U.S. operations in the Barents and Kara Seas where over 200 underground nuclear tests were conducted. The tests began in 1964 and the last one was conducted in 1990.

Other areas included the New Siberian Islands where Russian military bases were established, and in regions where many combined Naval/Civilian hydroacoustic, hydrographic, hydro-meteorological, hydrological, and ice-edge studies were being carried out. It also includes the research carried out on Soviet ice islands in the Arctic where Western submarines may have operated.

I wonder how the rapidly melting ice in the Arctic Ocean will affect the operations of Western and Russian submarines? The ice cover has always provided a relatively safe haven for submarines to operate virtually undetected as long as they are not communicating.

Significant development of new technology and equipment installed in the latest modern submarines of countries bordering the Arctic Ocean could allow for detection from surface, subsurface and space-based platforms.

If an Arctic agreement is signed, Fleets of each nation bordering the Arctic Ocean (with the exception of Russia) will have to build or acquire specially-equipped ice-strengthened ships and icebreakers to be able to protect and defend their sovereignty issues.

In 2004 Canada ratified the Law of the Sea Convention established by the United Nations in 1984. The agreement identifies those areas of the Arctic sea floor sectioned off to five circumpolar nations, Canada, the U.S., Russia, Denmark and Norway. One of the key issues in the future will certainly be control of the sea floor resources in the Arctic Ocean.

When the Law of the Sea issue is ratified, the Russians will have a formidable fleet of nuclear icebreakers to support and enforce its presence. If the ice fields recede as rapidly as scientists predict, it could mean that a new northern waterway would be open year round to vessels (a)using the Arctic as a direct Atlantic –Pacific route and (b) for petroleum/mineral mining extraction.

Nuclear-powered icebreakers such as the *Lenin* and the then 'new' Arktika-class icebreakers of the Soviet Ministry of the Merchant Fleet have made historic ventures into the thick Arctic ice, the Lenin since 1957. The *Arktika* was built at the Baltic Shipyards and operated in the Arctic until 2008. In 1977, it was the first surface vessel to reach the North Pole.

Three additional Arktika-class vessels followed: The *Sibir* from 1977 to 1992; the *Rossiya* (from 1985 to 2013), and the *Sovetsky Soyuz* from (1989 to 2010).

Two other Arktika-class nuclear-powered icebreakers, the *Yamal* (1992) and the *50 Let Pobedy* (50 Years of Victory -2007), the world's most powerful icebreaker, are still in operation.

In July 2013, the *Yamal* completed a rescue and evacuation of the Russian ice station NP-40 which had drifted into the Canadian Sector of the Arctic. A severe ice break-up in the ice forced the Russians to send the icebreaker on the 2200 mile journey into Canadian waters. According to an article in the Siberian Times on the 5 July 2013 the operation averted a risk of pollution in Arctic waters off the Canadian Coast.

This operation demonstrated that Russian nuclear-powered ice-breakers are capable of escorting their naval vessels to Soviet territorial boundaries penetrated by foreign vessels.

This enhanced capability, such as the combined use of the icebreaking carrier Sevmorput and the shallow draught *Taimyr* (1988) and *Vajgach* (1990), could also prove invaluable for:

- support to drifting ice stations and future petroleum platforms in the Arctic;

- search and rescue operations in an Arctic environment for both surface and sub-surface vessels;

- challenging non-Russian vessels and ice bases operating in the Soviet portion of the Arctic, and

- the establishment of a new northern passageway for escorting Soviet Merchant Fleet vessels between the Barents Sea and the Pacific Ocean

Since 1989, Russian tourist groups have also used the nuclear-powered vessels to carry tourists into the high Arctic. In 2008, the nuclear-powered icebreaker 'Fifty Years of Victory' carried up to 128 passengers to the North Pole on three different voyages.

It is significant to note that the Soviets currently have the largest fleet of nuclear-powered icebreakers in the world. In 2015, they are expected to launch the largest icebreaker in the world.

In retrospect, after learning about the Soviet advances in nuclear ice-breaking technology and their subsequent influence on the development of the Arctic, I was pleased with my decision in 1976 to produce a conference paper on the impact and the potential importance of the *Arktika* and the expansion of the Soviet Nuclear Icebreaker Fleet.

AUTHOR'S PERSPECTIVE

In the early 1970's, I conducted specialized research on Soviet Scientific Operations in the Arctic Ocean. I became aware of the significance of the area as a dividing line between North America and Asia. Ice and weather conditions dictated :

(a) the periods when ships could operate, and

(b) the life span of Soviet operations on Arctic ice-based platforms.

In an effort to learn all that I could about scientific operations in the Arctic, I visited local Libraries and read many scientific books and periodicals. I was impressed with the number of Soviet scientists involved and their range of scientific endeavors. I kept records on each of them. I was especially interested in those fields that had military implications.

Apart from the periodic transfer of submarines under the Arctic ice, and the suspicion that one of their Arctic ice bases was probably controlled by the Soviet Navy, the majority of the information was assessed as scientific/economic. Mapping of the Arctic Ocean was part of the process and eventually led to the naming of underwater ranges, the Mendeleev and Lomonosov Ridges. Little did I know that this would become one of the most contentious issues in the 21st Century surrounding the international boundaries to be set by the Law of the Sea Treaty regarding the Arctic Ocean.

When I was responsible for reporting on the development of the Soviet Nuclear Icebreaker Fleet it eventually became apparent that its role in support of Merchant Fleet activity in the Arctic would extend the Soviet shipping season. Eventually, we learned that the Icebreaker Fleet could also expand its role in support of Soviet naval operations, rescue missions and sorties to the North Pole and beyond.

Enter Vladimir Putin.

Although we could sense that all of these operations might result in some major changes in maritime operations in the Arctic Ocean, no one could have predicted the speed with which these events have happened. The delineation of international boundaries in the Arctic could be interpreted by the Russians in the same manner they treated boundaries in the Ukraine, and other former Soviet-dominated States in 2014-2015.

There is no doubt that Vladimir Putin will be in a position to use force to protect Russian claims to their side of the Arctic. That was made abundantly clear in 2013 when he opened a Russian naval base on Kotel'nyj Island on the New Siberian Islands.

POST-RETIREMENT RELATED INTERESTS/INCIDENTS

Meeting My Wife Merla

In 1991, I was fifty seven years old and lived in an apartment in Ottawa, Ontario. My two adult daughters had moved to Toronto but my widowed mother still resided in Ottawa. After my divorce, I met a few women but was not interested in getting married.

A friend of mine decided that she "could do better" in the female department. For an upcoming golf tournament at our club she suggested that one of her girlfriends be my partner. She said that Merla was a widow, lived alone in a large home in Nepean, Ontario and was the mother of three young adults, two daughters and a son.

At that time I had my own opinion about what type of partner I preferred. I suggested that we meet and decide about the golf tournament later. I told her that "most of the women I had dated were short and seemed to have a chip on their shoulder". Her friend "would have to be younger than me, at least five foot seven, and enjoy dancing and golf."

My friend replied; "She's forty eight, has a great personality, many friends, loves to dance and is very active in sports."

In a later conversation, Merla asked; "Does he smoke? Is he over fifty?"

"He doesn't smoke. And he loves to dance."

"He loves to dance. Great, but how old is he?"

"For goodness sake, it's only a date. You don't have to marry him!"

Merla agreed to meet me at our friend's home for birthday cake and coffee.

That night, I arrived early while Merla was half an hour late. I had my doubts about someone who would not have the courtesy to arrive on time. But she was charming, had a great smile and laugh - 'the real thing'.

Her apology: "I had pizza and watched a movie with friends at home, and I just had to see the end of the movie." Being a movie buff myself, I accepted her apology.

We agreed to participate in the golf tournament, which was advertised as a 'Mexican Night: Golf, Dine and Dance'. On our way out to our cars that night, I asked her if she wanted to 'dress up' like Mexicans. Merla was shocked to hear that this guy would want to dress up and happily accepted.

After golf on the night of our official date, we changed into our Mexican outfits and walked into the dance hall to encounter eighty-eight other golfers drinking marqueritas. Not one of them was wearing Mexican garb but they applauded our colourful attire.

We had a good laugh and enjoyed the evening. So referring to our earlier questions, "I got younger and she got taller!"

We were married on 25 July 1992 and have celebrated 'Christmas in July' for twenty three years.

Western Visitors to Communist Countries

During those years I worked at CSE and while I was travelling in Hungary, Russia, and Belarus after I retired, I learned how Communist countries treated diplomatic staff and visitors from western countries. Some were comical and others were scary.

When I worked at NSA in the early 1970s, I befriended an American who worked at the Agriculture Department. His job was to brief U.S. Agricultural Officers and Farm Groups who visited Communist countries for sales meetings.

He described the efforts by Warsaw Pact countries to get the upper hand on Western visitors and the methods they used to disrupt their lives. Late night phone calls by cranks and prostitutes, noises in the hallways, phone 'taps'and other 'dirty tricks' were only a few of the methods used.

Their goal was to keep the individual tired and on edge before the discussions began the next day.

I also met a few Canadian and American Attaches who had served at Embassies in Warsaw Pact countries. They had some interesting stories to tell.

They explained that their movements were limited to a specific distance from the city in which they lived. Military bases and scientific establishments were restricted to all foreigners. Attaches had to come up with unique methods to observe and photograph installations, buildings and military units of interest to the intelligence community.

In one instance, an Attache had curtains installed in his automobile so that no one could see who was inside. It also allowed him and/or his wife to photograph military or restricted installations through a small opening in the curtains as they drove by.

In Leningrad (now St. Petersburg) an American Attache and his family had picnics beside the Neva River. Occasionally, a submarine periscope could be observed moving through the channel enroute to the Baltic Sea. They would quickly gather the children near the river and were able to take their photos without arousing suspicion.

Some of the incidents were comical. Two friends of mine were sent to Moscow on a special mission at the Canadian Embassy. Being avid golfers, they had taken their golf clubs with them in hopes of playing in Europe when their operation was completed.

There was nowhere to practice hitting golf balls. So, one weekend they decided to go down to the river for a picnic. They took their irons and golf balls with them.

When they began to hit the balls into the river, a crowd gathered. As they continued to hit, the crowd increased.

Finally, when they were done, they noticed that the crowd was still there staring at the river. When they headed to their car, a Russian gentleman approached them and was scratching his head. In broken English he said, "Everyone is waiting to see how you will get the balls back."

Visit to Hungary, Slovakia and Czech Republic-1992

In 1992, Merla and I planned a European trip. Now that we were both retired, we decided to visit Denmark, Holland, Austria, France, Spain, Portugal and the former Iron Curtain countries, Hungary and the Czech

Republic. Czechoslovakia had recently been split into two separate Republics: the Czech Republic and Slovakia.

Because of my former background in intelligence, I contacted the Security Officer at the Communications Security Establishment Canada to check if I was allowed to visit the two former Soviet satellites. It was only two years since I had retired.

He advised us that it was safe to go.

We adopted our usual thorough approach and researched every aspect of the journey. We spent several months preparing for our six week holiday, ensuring that we had the appropriate clothing, currency and Eurail tickets. In addition to our Canadian passports, we needed only one Visa. That Visa was for a visit to the Czech Republic.

Our choice of airline, KLM, was predicated by the fact that we could fly from Canada to Europe and within Europe on one airline. We had obtained our Eurail passes to cover the shorter and more scenic routes.

After a week's visit in Holland and Denmark and another week in Vienna, Austria we took the hydrofoil to Budapest, Hungary. We liked Budapest and the people who were recently freed from the shackles of Communism. However, when we walked through the streets we were constantly confronted by shady characters trying to sell us anything and everything, and especially to exchange thousands of counterfeit Hungarian dollars for a fraction of their value.

On our last day in Budapest, we went to Keleti Train Station to obtain our sleeping car rail tickets for Prague in the Czech Republic. The clerk at the station examined our passports and Czech visas and issued us a sleeper ticket. She said it was a direct route to Prague.

We arrived at the train station at 8:30 p.m. The Keleti Station was a zoo. One was constantly being accosted for handouts, money exchanges and rooms for rent. Regular citizens warned us to stay away from the area at night, to keep our money out of sight and as close to our body as possible and to watch our luggage at all times.

We managed to get through the maze of beggars and money-changers and boarded the train at 8:45, a half-hour before departure. We settled into our small compartment and talked with a young American couple who were going to Prague before heading to Berlin to run in the Berlin Marathon. The train left on time. We were on our way.

As we talked, the train conductor picked up our Eurail passes, overnight tickets and passports complete with the visas for the Czech Republic. We were reluctant to hand him our passports for fear we would never see them again. It was a feeling we got each time we handed them to hotel clerks and train conductors. Without a passport in Europe, you are virtually helpless.

We settled in to our tiny, stuffy two-cot compartment, undressed down to our underwear and read some of the travel material on Prague.

An hour later, the train stopped for about two minutes. We weren't aware that there was a stop, but presumed it was the point at which the Austrian Border Guards and Customs officials boarded the train. We had become accustomed to the entourage of personnel who boarded the trains, so we weren't surprised to see the drug-sniffing dogs go through our car.

A few minutes later there was a knock on the door of our compartment but before we could cover ourselves the door was flung open. We scrambled to put on some clothes. My wife was very embarrassed at being caught partially naked in front of two soldiers standing in the doorway.

From their uniforms, I couldn't tell if they were Hungarian or Austrian. But my eyes were glued to the large pistols in their holsters.

The big burly one had our passports and our Czech visas in his hand. "Where …you…go?"

"To Prague," I answered.

"Visas !" he responded coldly.

"You have them in your hand," I said, watching the train conductor as he paced impatiently behind the two soldiers.

"No, Slovak visas,"

"Oh, we're not going to Slovakia, just to Prague in the Czech Republic," my wife answered confidently.

The soldier pointed his finger towards the floor. "Is Slovakia! Visas!"

Merla and I stared at each other, dumbfounded.

I answered, "That's impossible. We asked for a direct train from Budapest to Prague.

There was no other city or country mentioned on the Eurail schedule we used at the train station."

We had assumed that the train went through Austria. The clerk at Keleti Station saw our passports and Czech visas. She neither asked for nor told us we needed Slovakian visas, otherwise we would have taken the train to Vienna.

Neither soldier spoke English, so the train conductor translated for us. I was never sure what he said and he wouldn't answer any questions I asked him about our predicament. He was obviously upset about the situation, possibly because we were holding up the entire train. He subsequently proved to be a sneaky and unreliable go-between.

The burly officer listened to the conductor, turned to us and said, "American?"

"No, Canadians." My wife pointed to the Canadian flag on our backpacks and the passports.

I asked the conductor to tell the soldier that we were only going to Prague for three days and we had bought these seats for the overnight trip which we thought would go through Austria. I added that we didn't want to get off the train until we reached Prague.

I don't know what the conductor said to him, but the soldier's face flushed and he glared at us. I wonder if he was angered by the fact we weren't going to visit his country.

That was when we became concerned for our safety. I had earlier noticed about twenty other soldiers on or around the train. Most were carrying automatic weapons. Some were checking under and above the railcars. For some unknown reason, I thought about the Gestapo and recalled the WW2 movies where these encounters had occurred. Though I was nervous, I tried to keep my cool.

I had another problem I certainly couldn't discuss with any of them: the fact that I had been employed in a highly classified position in an intelligence organization within the Canadian Department of National Defence.

It would not be prudent to place myself in a position where they would discover that fact. So, I had to remain calm and not create an incident.

"Passport, 90 days, Czech Republic."

I figured that was the problem.He thought we were staying in the Czech Republic for 90 days.

I told the conductor "That's what the Czech Embassy allows for every visitor. It only means that one must leave after ninety days. It's the maximum level. We have four more countries to visit and we have reserved KLM tickets from Lisbon to Canada on 21 October. We're only going to Prague for three or four days."

The conductor translated for us. An animated discussion took place. The soldier only frowned and walked away. I was suspicious of the conductor's true motives for getting the problem resolved.

"What did he say?" I asked.

He didn't reply. They walked down the corridor together leaving us all alone. We hurried to pull on the rest of our clothes.

The young American couple walked out of their compartment. "Is everything okay with you folks?"

My wife said, "What will we do? We're out in the middle of nowhere, we traded in all of our Hungarian money at the station, we have no place to stay and it's almost midnight. They just can't leave us here." I pulled out the Eurail train schedule and checked it again. It only showed a trip from Budapest to Prague. We had no recourse but to wait.

Ten minutes later, the train began to move. The ordeal was over, but we wouldn't feel comfortable until we had reached Prague and had our passports in our hands.

Call it instinct, intuition or 'Murphy's Law', but for some unknown reason we decided not to undress again on the train. We soon learned to trust our instincts.

Twenty minutes later the train came to a stop. In the darkness, we could see the outline of what appeared to be an old train station. There were several soldiers dispersed on both sides of the tracks, surrounding the train. Many were toting sub-machine guns. Some were checking under the rail cars and others were standing on the roofs.

There was a knock on the door. We recoiled at the sound. When I opened the door, the two soldiers and the conductor were standing there.

"Visas," said the soldier, handing us two completely different blank forms to fill out. One was in English and the other in German.

Despite our trembling hands and fumbling fingers, we wrote quickly. I filled out the German form (in English) by copying what my wife had put down in the appropriate spaces on her form.

When we handed them to the soldier, he said "Photos!"

I said, "No photographs. We don't carry photographs around with us for these purposes. Look at the photographs on the Czech visas."

He frowned. "No good."

They all left again. I cornered the conductor, who by now I considered nothing less than a weasel. He had done nothing for us nor shown any feelings or compassion for our predicament. He turned his head and walked away.

They returned fifteen minutes later.

"Leave train. Go back to Budapest," said the soldier, nothing more than that.

I said, "Why are you treating us this way? We are Canadians. My son-in-law's parents were born in Slovakia. We are friends with the Czech and Slovak people. We help people all over the world. We didn't know the train was going through Slovakia or we would have bought Slovak visas. We bought Czech visas. It cost us $120.00. We aren't scheduled to get off the train until we reach Prague. We paid a lot of money for the sleeping car and we have no Hungarian money or a room to stay in Budapest."

The weasel got into another animated discussion with the soldier. I could sense that all he wanted to do was to get his train moving. He couldn't care less what they did to us.

"Leave now!" said the soldier.

My wife and I looked at each other helplessly. We knew we had no choice.

"Okay," I said, throwing my hands in the air. We weren't about to argue with the entire Slovakian Army.

The other soldier, who had watched the exchanges between us and his obvious higher-ranking officer, looked at us sheepishly. It appeared to me that he saw this older couple, one completely gray and looking close to his sixty years, were not the type of people he would consider a threat to him or his country.

I gave it one more shot, trying to appeal to their sensitive side. "Look, I know you are only doing your job, but we are harmless citizens on a vacation."

The burly soldier was becoming impatient. "You leave."

I turned to the conductor, contempt in my eyes, "Where's our passports and rail tickets?"

"When you leave the train."

We gathered our bags and left the compartment. The second soldier grabbed my heavy backpack and carried it off the train for me.

I was astounded at the number of soldiers that were under and on top of the train.

When I reached the platform, I turned around and realized that my wife wasn't there!

I walked back to the steps of the train and waited. I was becoming very concerned for her safety. A few moments later – it felt like an hour - she appeared at the top of the steps. I helped her down the stairs.

"My God, I was worried," I said, hugging her hard.

"I'm sorry, but just as I was leaving the American couple came to their door and gave me some of their left-over Forint. They wanted us to have some Hungarian currency when we arrived back in Budapest."

I caught their eye in the window of their compartment and waved a 'thank you' to them. We had their address and would write them a letter when we got back to Canada.

The old wooden platform was dark and dirty. We stood alone in the cold night air on the centre platform between two sets of tracks. A few people were standing in front of a dilapidated wooden train station. I saw the conductor and walked up to him.

"Here's your Eurail passes. The guards have your passports."

I checked the tickets, but the ones for the overnight trip to Prague were not included.

"Wait a minute. Where are the tickets for the trip to Prague? If we won't be able to use them, we want them back so we can get a refund when we return to Budapest."

"No tickets," said the conductor.

If I had been a violent man, I could have strangled him right there on the spot, regardless of the presence of twenty or so soldiers that were around us.

Twenty minutes later, the train going to Hungary arrived. Merla and I vowed that we wouldn't board until we had our passports. We sat on the wooden bench, determined that they would have to drag us onto the train.

Our fears were alleviated a few minutes later when we saw the second soldier walking towards us, waving our passports and motioning for us to board. He handed us our passports, shrugged his shoulders and nudged us onto the train.

We were not prepared for what we saw. The trains of Europe we had encountered were clean, bright and comfortable. This train was not only the dirtiest one we had ever been on, but it had food and other debris strewn all over the floor. Two empty beer bottles rattled from one side to the other. The stench was unbearable. The toilets (WC) were filthy and blocked up. We could hardly breathe when we used them.

When the train pulled out, we had an empty feeling in our stomachs and deep bitterness over the whole incident made worse by that despicable conductor. The only redeeming factor was we were unharmed and a major confrontation was averted.

During the trip back to Budapest we encountered feelings of anxiety, helplessness, frustration and bitterness. When we left Keleti Train Station, it was daytime; we didn't know what to expect at 1:00 in the morning.

We looked over our *Let's Go Europe* book to get some idea where we could call for a room that night. We knew that at that time of the morning it would be difficult, almost next to impossible. We were bracing ourselves for the worst…the possibility of spending the night in the train station.

At Keleti Station, a few passengers left the train and we fell in behind them. Our first plan was to head for the telephones. Except for a few vagrants lying on the benches along the side of the tracks, the station was virtually deserted. We sighed with relief. Three telephone booths were situated on the bottom floor.

My wife got on the phone and began dialing the phone numbers of the hotels we had selected from the travel book. While she was talking to one of the hotel staff, I noticed a man waiting on one side of the booth.

Before long he was joined by two other men. They stood around in a circle, occasionally glancing our way. I couldn't understand why they were waiting. The two other phones were available. I realized that we were alone! Isolated!

I put my head into the booth and said, "Hang up, quick!"

My wife said, "Wha..what's the matter."

I slammed the phone into its cradle. "Grab your backpack and follow me."

She noticed the three men as we headed for the escalator.

I shouted to an imaginary friend, "Hey, Bill! Bill Dawson! We're down here! Wait up for us."

Merla followed me, her mouth agape. She whispered, "What… who's Bill Dawson?"

"No one. I saw those men loitering around while you were on the phone. I had to make them think that we weren't alone."

Her eyes opened wide. "Good move, sweetheart."

On the escalator, we glanced back to see how the three men had reacted. They watched us until we were out of sight. We walked quickly towards the large waiting room at the other end of the station. We would be safer there. It was well lit and I could see people entering the room.

Inside, we found people lying on the floor, sprawled across benches or curled up wherever they could find a niche. It was evident that most of them were drifters, vagrants, beggars and every other type of low life who needed a place to sleep for the night. There was no place to sit, so we dropped our bags against the wall and checked out the situation.

This indeed was a zoo, a scary zoo! But, I felt that there was safety in numbers. It was far better to be in here than *out there* where one could get cornered and no one would know about it.

I had to get to a phone and there were none in the area. My wife was very nervous. Despite my own fears, I reassured her that it was safe. I would go outside and find a phone. I hugged her, gave her a kiss and headed for the door.

Inside the station, a man at a magazine kiosk told me in broken English that the Central Post Office next door was open all night and had pay telephones. In addition, there were police inside.

Keleti station had the usual group of taxi drivers loitering around the exit, but these particular taxi drivers were far from normal. They were openly aggressive and downright rude. As soon as I exited the station through the doors, they were on me like a pack of wolves.

"You want taxi?"

"You want to exchange money?"

"I have nice room. 'Pension ….cheap."

"You need woman for the night, nice, clean young girl, seventeen?"

"No, thanks!" I had witnessed these scenes before on many previous trips to Europe on my own. So, I did what I always do.

I looked towards the Post Office on my right, raised my hand and shouted, "Hey, Bill, Bill Dawson, I'm over here."

I headed towards the Post Office, their curses ringing out behind me.

About halfway from the building, I noticed a man loitering near the station wall on the other side of the street. Moments later, I heard a pinging sound on the stone wall above his head, then another.

I began to run towards the building. I had recognized the sound of an Air Gun or a Pistol, so I ran as fast as I could towards the Post Office.

When I reached the door to the Post Office, I was met by two Hungarian Politizia. I explained that I needed to use the phone and told them about the shooting incident at the Train Station.

They threw up their arms, shrugged their shoulders and replied in broken English, "We protect here! No police go over there!"

I thought, *'Oh thanks, that makes me feel better! I was sure happy my wife didn't know about this'.*

Once inside, I called the all-night Hungarian IBUSZ reservation office. I couldn't believe it. We finally got a break. They got us a room, gave us directions and an estimate on the cost of the cab fare.

For more than one reason, I raced back across the square keeping my eyes and ears alert for any further signs of what I thought to be bullets from a pistol or an air gun. I broke through the 'cabbie barricade' and headed for the waiting room.

Merla was standing in the doorway.

"What's wrong?" I asked.

"I just couldn't stay in there. The stench was overwhelming and this creep moved close to me and kept staring in my direction. Even though I put on my aggressive/assertive look, my imagination was in overdrive. I was fighting panic. How long should I stay here before I go looking for you? What if I can't find you? I kept thinking- Please don't let us be part of a 'Holiday Disappearance'. Then, I thought, My God, we're 10,000 miles from home and all alone."

I grabbed her and gave her a big hug. "Get your backpack. We have a room."

For the first time since we left the train, she was able to smile.

We picked up our backpacks and headed towards the exit. Though I knew we had to get a cab, I dreaded the fact that I would have to expose her to the creeps waiting outside.

When we exited, they were around us like flies at a waste dump.

"Room, room, you want a room?"

A large framed overweight man, obviously one of the leaders of the group, walked over and stood right in front of me. He dragged on his cigarette and spoke out of the corner of his mouth. "I have a better room, bigger and cheaper. You take this room."

"No thanks, we have a room." I turned to the cabbie beside him and said "We need a taxi to get to our hotel right now. We have to go to the Buda side, near the Castle. I understand that it should cost about 70 to 80 Forints."

He sipped the coffee in his Styrofoam cup and spoke to his friends in Hungarian. They all laughed.

"Hah. 140 Forints! No take our room, cost 140 Forints."

I turned around and offered the same price to the other seven or eight cabbies, but they just grinned and laughed. I assumed that the cab drivers in Budapest must be pretty wealthy. Otherwise, why would they hang around an empty train station at 1:00 a.m. when there were no trains scheduled to arrive for another five hours-and refuse a fare!

Merla and I looked at each other and, without hesitation, grabbed our backpacks and headed across the empty square. We heard the grumbling behind us. I wasn't sure how they would react. I kept glancing back to see if any of them were following us or if they had gone to their cars.

The leader shouted, "You big shot. You walk to Buda!" The others roared with laughter. But they didn't follow us.

We could accept the insult.

When we reached the other side of the square, we were surprised and relieved when we saw another taxicab coming towards us. We hailed it. The driver was a young man, clean-shaven and neatly dressed.

"Can you take us to Buda? We can pay you 100 Forints."

He spoke a little English. "Yes."

After helping us to load our backpacks into the trunk, we were on our way. Within 15 minutes we were standing at the door of the Pension. We paid the driver and also gave him all of our leftover Austrian change.

Relieved and exhausted, we slept well that night.

The next morning, we returned to Keleti Station and took a train to Salzburg, Austria. We didn't get our money back for the train fare. Although we never made it to Prague, we met a wonderful Australian couple, and toured Austria and Germany together.

Perhaps we will journey to Prague and the Czech Republic some day, but I doubt that we would ever have the desire to return to Slovakia.

After returning to Canada, we learned that when Czechoslovakia split into the Czech and Slovak Republics, Canada declared that both Republics would require separate Visas in order to visit Canada. As a result, both Republics demanded separate Visas for Canadians to visit *their* Countries. I found it interesting that the United States had, as of 1993, not imposed the same conditions on the two new Republics.

Belarus and Russia-2001

To ensure that I had conformed to the required waiting period designated by CSE, before visiting a Communist country, I contacted the CSE Security Officer and gave him our itinerary. Belarus and Russia were included in the list of several countries we would be visiting. He confirmed that there would be no problem.

Merla and I personally encountered a number of unusual incidents during the guided bus tour, one in Belarus and two in Moscow.

When our bus arrived at the border between Poland and Belarus, we had to hand our passports over to our Russian tour guide. He visited the local Immigration Office and was gone for quite a long time.

Besides Merla and I, there was one other Canadian on the trip. When our guide returned he said that there was a delay because of a Canadian passport. My first thought was 'It has to be me'.

I was surprised. According to our External Affairs Department all we needed was a valid passport. I began to worry that this would turn into an incident and they would find out where I had been employed.

As it turned out, the other Canadian, a woman, was the one they were looking for. For some unknown reason she had no passport. She was married to an American who had died and didn't renew her Canadian passport. All she had was her driver's licence. She only had to fill out a special form and they allowed her to enter the country. I sighed with relief.

We finally got through Belarus and arrived in Moscow two days later.

When we arrived at our hotel in Moscow, we had to declare how much money we had brought into the country. In order to conform to Russian law, we were required to fill in a form on the day we departed, stating how much money we were taking out of the country. Visitors would have to pay a tax if the total exceeded the allowed limit.

We learned that there was a casino in our hotel so one evening we retrieved our passports from the front desk, joined our friends and headed for the casino. We noticed four or five burly men in dark suits. Were they from the Federal Security Services (FSB), formerly the KGB?

After several hours of me losing and my wife winning, we decided our fun was over for the night. Our friend, however, wanted to continue with her winning streak. We figured she would be safe, with the FSB around.

After returning our passports to the front desk, we headed up the stairs to the elevators. As we approached the elevators to our left, a heavy-set man in a dark suit said, "No, not here. You tourists, you go to the right, to the other elevators."

It appeared to us that the FSB tried to isolate foreigners from the regular Russian citizens staying at the hotel.

We never had access to our passports while in Russia, but we were able to talk to the citizens we met along the route, with a Russian escort not too far away.

One of the highlights was driving right by the entrance to the KGB Headquarters. Later, at a Russian War Memorial, I posed with a group of young Russian recruits (see image 35).

We also took many photos of St. Basil's and Red Square (see image 36). as well as the gargantuan GUM Department Store. Another surprising highlight was the majestic Moscow Underground Subway system: the murals on the walls were astounding- and, there was no graffiti whatsoever! The lineups for Lenin's Tomb were too long. We were pleasantly surprised that the temperature was seventy-five degrees Fahrenheit.

Finally, our group gathered to walk through the Kremlin. As I approached the entrance, odd things were going through my mind.

Would they have my name on a list of people who worked at the National Security Agency or the Canadian Embassy in Washington? Did they have records on personnel who worked at CSE that could be flagged by the scanning of our passports?

All these thoughts disappeared when I walked through the arches and into the Kremlin. It was surreal, definitely a highlight of our trip for me. We took photos of Terem Palace (see image 37) and the largest bell in the world, the Tsar Bell (see image 38). Just being on those grounds was something special.

I am still amazed that, after being employed by CSE, two of the things I thought could never have been possible, actually happened: visiting the Russian Embassy in Ottawa and the Kremlin in Moscow.

On another occasion, while wandering around Red Square, we were constantly harassed by people trying to sell us used military hats with insignias, packages of post cards and booklets. I bought a hat with a KGB logo. The vendors looked very poor.

One of them followed us to our bus, trying to get a last minute sale. He stood there while we all embarked.

A vehicle drove right up to the bus and I recognized it as a police car. The officer opened the window and hailed the vendor. After a long discussion, we watched the poor vendor reach into his pocket and hand the officer a wad of bills.

Someone commented that they were not allowed to sell anything in the bus areas.

I decided to pull a prank on my fellow tour passengers. On our last day in Moscow, I made up a sign, put on the KGB hat and persuaded our tour guide to meet me at the bus before the rest of the group arrived.

The sign read: "Departure tax, $5 Rubles per person".

We took an overnight train from Moscow to St. Petersburg our next destination. The highlight was the Hermitage Museum. It was so large that we only covered a small portion of the celebrated Russian treasures. On a 'free' afternoon in St. Petersburg, Merla and I visited the Soviet Cruiser Kirov Memorial (see 1mage 39) and walked around the streets near our hotel. Driving past the Arctic and Antarctic Scientific Research Institute (AANII), no one could have imagined how exciting it was for me.

35. Meeting Young Russian Recruits in Moscow

36. Red Square with St. Basil's Church in Background

37. Terem Palace in Red Square

38. View of Tsar Bell from inside the Kremlin

39. Soviet Cruiser Kirov Memorial in St Petersburg

Visit to Scotland/Orkney Islands-2005

During our month long visit to Scotland in September 2005 we decided to go to the Orkney Islands. We visited a rather unique museum, the Orkney Wireless Museum, in the city of Kirkwall.

It is an interesting museum featuring domestic and amateur radio equipment and some unique items used to disguise radios. Some of the equipment bore a similarity to the type used at our Canadian intercept sites.

I was intrigued and excited to see an Enigma cipher machine used by the Germans during WW2.

I would recommend the museum to anyone who has been involved in the technical side of intelligence collection.

China-2007

On our visit to China in 2007, I was surprised when our Chinese National Tour Guide told me that he had been an Intelligence Officer in the Chinese Navy. We had some interesting conversations during the three weeks we were with him. Of course, the discussions were all carried out while we were outside, away from people, buildings and the like. Surprisingly, we were able to walk anywhere and mix in with the Chinese citizens at any time of day or night.

Barbara Blaney – A Canadian Intelligence Pioneer

In 1999, my wife Merla and I moved to a condominium in the town of Carleton Place, Ontario, southwest of Ottawa, Canada. Little did I know that I would cross paths with Barbara Blaney (nee Sinclair), a resident in our building. Barbara was one of the first members of an intelligence operation that spawned the current SIGINT organization represented by CSE.

Although we had often talked to each other on a number of occasions neither Barbara nor I discussed where we had worked in the past. In August 2013, I finally sat down with her to learn more about her appointment and her duties. We compared our experiences, particularly the efforts not to reveal the true nature of our work.

She was recruited in 1942, one of approximately 800 Canadians, to work with William Stephenson who was setting up a highly secretive organization in New York City. Her father opposed her move but her mother supported her decision. Two weeks later she moved to New York.

She had little or no idea about the work she was assigned or the significance of the product she was about to produce. Several Canadian women were hired; Barbara Blaney was one of them.

Canadian-born industrialist William Stephenson had served with the Canadian Armed Forces during WWll and was subsequently selected by Winston Churchill to head up the New York operations. Though he was named by Churchill as the Head of the British Passport Control Office, when the U.S. entered the war, he became British Security Coordinator for the Western hemisphere. It included MI6, the UK Secret Intelligence Service as well as MI5, Military Intelligence and the Special Operations Executive (SOE) at Rockefeller Centre.

His Unit worked closely with the FBI and the OSS (Office of Strategic Services), predecessor of the CIA, to set up an aggressive intelligence program responsible for relaying valuable intelligence intercepted on Japanese communications and passing it to Canadian/UK/US code-breakers.

Stephenson referred to intelligence collection as 'a Spyglass, the importance of knowing what the enemy was doing, spying out the facts, the truth'.

Barbara soon found out that her job involved decoding Japanese cipher messages and was given a two week course. The Centre operated 24 hours a day for 7 days a week.

After the war, Stephenson was given knighthood by the British and received the Distinguished Flying Cross. The government of France honoured him with the Croix de Guerre. He was immortalized in the novel and movie 'A Man Called Intrepid'. Stephenson died in January1989, only a few months before the Berlin Wall was torn down.

Mrs. Blaney was sworn to secrecy and, until 2012, never revealed the nature of her work.

In 2013, at the age of 96, she was honoured by CSE and the British Government for her vital service performed during WWll. This all came about after a discussion with a friend who was working in a high Canadian government position. That information was passed to CSE.

At a special 'Tea with Mrs. Blaney' on 17 April 2013 hosted by CSE, Mrs. Blaney was presented with a plaque and certificate by the Deputy Chief of Information Technology Security (see image 40). The CSE award also stated that 'Some of Mrs. Blaney's duties involved working on 5 letter codes'.

She also received a plaque from the British Government Code and Cypher School (see image 41) signed by David Cameron, the British Prime Minister and a Certificate of Service from British Security Coordination (see image 42) signed by William Stephenson.

I met with Barbara (see image 43) on a couple of occasions to discuss our experiences. As of September 2014, Barbara Blaney still resides in Carleton Place.

I often shake my head when I realize that it took almost 70 years to recognize her contribution, but at least she finally got it!

40. CSE Award to Barbara Blaney

41. Award from British Code School signed by PM Cameron

42. Award from British Security Services signed by William Stephenson

43. Author Ron Lawruk and Barbara Blaney

ACKNOWLEDGEMENTS TO:

CSE, NSA, GCHQ for their cooperation and to all of those officers with whom I worked in all of the intelligence organizations for their input to this book.

LIST OF ABBREVIATIONS AND ACRONYMS USED IN THIS BOOK

AARI	Arctic and Antarctic Research Institute
AANII	Arctic and Antarctic Scientific Research Institute
CANUKUS	Canada, United Kingdom, United States
CANSLO/W	Canadian Senior Liaison Office, Washington, D.C.
CBNRC	Communications Branch, National Research Council
CCGS	Canadian Coast Guard Service
CFS	Canadian Forces Station
CFSRS	Canadian Forces Supplementary Radio System
CIA	Central Intelligence Agency
CIS	Chief, Intelligence Services, Canada
CO	Communications Officer
CSE	Communications Security Establishment, Canada
CSIS	Canadian Security and Intelligence Services, Canada
DDI	Directorate of Defence Intelligence, Canada
DSTI	Directorate of Scientific and Technical Intelligence, Canada

GCHQ	Government Communications Headquarters, UK
HMCS	Her Majesty's Canadian Ship
KGB	Committee for State Security, Russia (now FSB)
MARCOM	Maritime Command Headquarters Halifax, Nova Scotia
NFOIO	Naval Field Operational Intelligence Office, USA
NOSIC	Naval Ocean Surveillance Intelligence Center, USA
NP-12	North Pole -12, Soviet Arctic Ice Base
NSR	Northern Sea Route
OPEN SKIES	International Treaty involving unarmed overflight inspections of NATO/Warsaw Pact countries
SIGINT	Signals Intelligence

ABOUT THE AUTHOR

Ron Lawruk was born in Ottawa, Canada on 29 March 1934. Except for the one year that he worked in Calgary, Alberta and three years in Washington, D.C., he has lived either in or near the Ottawa area.

He attended Canadian Martyrs Catholic School and completed Junior Matriculation at St. Patrick's College in Ottawa East in 1952.

His first job was as a bookkeeper/accountant with Spartan Air Services, an aerial photography firm in Ottawa where he worked until 1957. That year he was promoted to Accountant/Office Manager of the Spartan office located in Calgary, Alberta.

In February1958, he left Spartan to return to Ottawa where he was employed by Canadian Aero Service Ltd.

In May 1958, Ron was hired by the Communications Branch, National Research Council (CBNRC), now the Communications Security Establishment Canada, (CSE).

H spent thirty two years with CBNRC/CSE, three of which were as a Canadian Liaison Officer at the National Security Agency (NSA) in Maryland, USA from 1968 to 1971 and five years as the CSE Liaison Officer at the Canadian National Defence Headquarters in Ottawa.

He and his wife Merla live in Carleton Place, a small town outside Ottawa since 1998 and spend five months a year in their home in Mesa, Arizona. Together they have four daughters, one son and five fabulous grandsons.

After retiring in 1990, Ron decided to fulfill his dream to become an author.

His first attempt at writing novels actually began while he was working at NSA in the late 1960s. Ron had become enthralled by the exploits of the infamous Russian spies in England. He ravenously read all of the published books about spies in the Library.

In the 1980s, terrorism began to spread in Europe and Asia. He expanded his research to include the roots, origin and expansion of worldwide terrorism. Tom Clancy became his favorite contemporary author.

Considering his background in intelligence, Ron researched all of the open source material on the Russian spy system controlled by the KGB. In 1986, He had finally devised a plot but needed a plausible story.

He needed a main character, something different, so he made the spy a woman, a Russian woman. Now, how would he introduce her?

That's where Ron's knowledge of the Russian system kicked in. Why not make her a daughter of a Russian Foreign Service Officer who is trained as a spy for the KGB?

Next, he wanted her to meet and seduce a Senator running for President of the United States. How does he get them to meet? Why not create another character, a U.S. woman whom the Senator meets, courts and plans to marry.

Now, where and how do they train spies in Russia? How does he exchange the Russian woman for the American woman? That's enough information!

Ron's first full length novel was titled *A Spy Too Close*.

In *A Spy Too Close*, since he was more familiar with the locations and activities of intelligence operations in Canada, he needed a Canadian character in his book. So, he introduced a fictitious character, Matt Maloney of the Royal Canadian Mounted Police.

The RCMP was undergoing a change in its mandate at that time and the Canadian Security and Intelligence Service was being formed to separate the Federal 'Police' duties from the 'Intelligence and Security' responsibilities. Ron decided to make him a CSIS agent, a counterpart of the United States' Central Intelligence Agency (CIA).

A Spy Too Close was published in 2005 and was still his most popular seller into 2014.

It was followed by his second novel, *Alliance of Terror*, published in 2009. Ron began writing 'Alliance' in the late 1980s; his first choice for a title was 'The Domino Alliance'. Matt Maloney, now collaborating with the FBI, confronts a team of foreign terrorists operating in the western U.S. It is uncanny how 'Alliance' closely resembled the terrorist attacks on the United States on 9/11/2001, some 20 years later!

If Words Could Kill, the third and final novel in the Trilogy, is a political thriller set in the first term of Barack Obama's Presidency. It involves a plot by Democrats in the White House, State Department and the CIA, to eliminate foreign media opposed to the Obama government.

The press release of 'Words' was published in the Washington magazine 'Politico'. Ron was contacted by one of their reporters (see image 44) and asked to appear on their 'live' Web broadcast the following morning in Washington to discuss the premise of the novel.

However, Ron was unable to arrange for a flight in time to meet their scheduled program the next morning. Unfortunately, the Politico staff became involved in U.S. election coverage and their interest in the story waned.

From: "Christine Delargy" <christine.delargy@cbsinteractive.com>
To: <carpaediem2@rogers.com>
Sent: Monday, October 18, 2010 3:26 PM
Subject: CBS News request
Hi-

Patrick Gavin was kind enough to pass along your email address. We have a daily political webcast called "Washington Unplugged" and feature various authors and new books. You can check out the show here- chsnews.com/washingtonunplugged

We'd be interested in doing an interview with you on "If Words Could Kill." We tape daily at 12:30pmET from the DC bureau-2020 M St. NW. Bob Schieffer, John Dickerson and various CBS correspondents host the webcast

Let me know if this is something you'd be interested and we can make arrangements from there.

Thank you!

--
Christine Delargy
CBS News- Washington, DC
O 202-457-4426
C 202-736-0768

Politico invitation for 'live' Web interview

Ron has published four other books:

A children's story titled *A Bark is Worse than a Bite* in 2007. The story- told by the dog named Bark- is about an attempted burglary of his owner's home and how he becomes a hero;

A Funny Thing Happened on My Way to Puberty in 2008; four short stories about teenagers (circa the 1940's);

For Love and Country- A Canadian Soldiers Story in 2011; a true life biography about a WWII Soldier's bout with Post Traumatic Stress Disorder (PTSD);

Murder in the Resort: Six Short Stories also published in 2011, featuring 'Murder in the Resort'; 'Courage of the Damned'; 'Food For Thought'; 'The Bend'; 'The Last Hurrahs'; and 'Journey of Fear';

All of Ron Lawruk's books are available on Amazon and Kindle. 'Journey of Fear' was one of the stories in *Murder in the Resort*. It was a real life experience that Ron and his wife Merla encountered in Slovakia in 1992.

Ron Lawruk's Published Books

A Spy Too Close, originally Bondi Studios
(Amazon.com and KINDLE, Fiction)

In 1988, the Russians devise a plot to plant a woman spy in the White House.

Matt Maloney, a Canadian Security Intelligence Officer from CSIS and an FBI agent team up in pursuit of the spy and her protective Russian assassin from eastern Canada through New York State to Washington, D.C.

The story offers a number of twists and turns as the spy seduces a senior official of the CIA and the U.S. Senator, a Democrat running for the Presidency.

Alliance of Terror, originally Bondi Studios
(Amazon.com and KINDLE, Fiction)

Matt Maloney, a Counter-Terrorist expert now working for the FBI in Washington, D.C. is involved in a search for a notorious international terrorist in California. He tracks him to a secret terrorist training camp in the San Jacinto Mountains.

Tipped off by an undercover British MI-5 informant in the international Freedom Fighters Alliance, Maloney learns of a plot involving targets in the USA.

He and his FBI team race to deter and apprehend the terrorists the terrorists before they attack Los Angeles, San Diego, New York, Washington and many other U.S. cities and military establishments.

In an exciting climax, he and his FBI team engage the terrorists on a small island off the coast of South Carolina.

If Words Could Kill, originally Bondi Studios
(Amazon.com and KINDLE, Fiction)

After riding the crest of unprecedented popularity of the Democratic President of the USA, loyal State Department and CIA Democrats encounter increased scrutiny and criticism.

U.S. diplomacy and prestige in the world is waning. Domestic issues such as the economy, Town Hall meetings, the Health Care program and failing bank systems cloud the Democratic Party programs.

To stem the tide of rising anti-USA articles by the international media, Senior Democrats in the White House, the State Department and the CIA concoct a deadly plan to curb their criticism.

Two women, an employee of the State Department and a political writer for the Washington Times discover the plot and contact Matt Maloney at the FBI.

In the exciting conclusion, the two women and Maloney confront the hired assassins and expose the White House and State Department Democrats behind the scheme.

Murder in the Resort, originally Bondi Studios
(Amazon.com, Amazon.ca and Kindle, Fiction & Non-Fiction)

Six short stories in this book about life will make you smile and bring tears to your eyes:

Courage of the Damned: A rookie pitcher for the Los Angeles Dodgers learns that he has a life-threatening disease on the eve of his World Series debut. Fiction

Food For Thought: While visiting Bar Harbor, Maine on a summer vacation a young boy demonstrates an uncommon compassion for an elderly woman. Non-Fiction

Journey of Fear: The author and his wife were ejected from a train in the middle of the night by Slovakian soldiers; Non-Fiction.

The Bend: A young couple visit an old hotel and get more than they bargained for; Fiction/non-Fiction.

The Last Hurrahs: The last years of an aging woman and how she maintained her poise and humour while she coped with Alzheimers; Non-Fiction.

Murder in the Resort: A tongue-in-cheek story about a murder in Mesa, Arizona which disrupted the lives of the residents of the Diamond Point Resort; Fiction.

For Love and Country, A Canadian Soldier's Story, originally Bondi Studios
(Amazon.com; Amazon.ca and Kindle; Biography)

This is the true life story of Private Ted Patrick who served with the Irish Regiment of Canada in Italy and Holland during the Second World War and his bout with Post-Traumatic Stress Disorder.

Additional information is available at Ron's website: www.ronlawruk.com

Printed in Canada